D0807296

THE LONGER

THE LONGER RUN

A Daughter's Story of Arthur Wint

Valerie Wint

IAN RANDLE PUBLISHERS

Kingston • *Miami*

First published in Jamaica, 2012 by
Ian Randle Publishers
11 Cunningham Avenue
Box 686
Kingston 6
www.ianrandlepublishers.com

© 2012, Valerie Wint

National Library of Jamaica Cataloguing in Publication Data

Wint, Valerie
    The longer run : a daughter's story of Arthur Wint / Valerie Wint

    p. : ill.; cm.

ISBN 978-976-637-518-8 (pbk)

1. Wint, Arthur, 1920-1992   2. Athletes – Jamaica – Biography
I. Title

796.42092   dc 22

All rights reserved. No part of this publication may be reproduced, stored in a retrieval system, or transmitted in any form, or by any means electronic, photocopying, recording or otherwise without prior permission of the author or publisher.

Cover and book design by Ian Randle Publishers
Cover image courtesy of Lauren Bauer
Printed in United States of America

Table of Contents

Foreword

It was more than six decades ago and yet I can still remember every moment of that unforgettable evening in August, as we gathered on the family verandah in Hanover, straining to listen to the short wave BBC Broadcast from London. Above the intermittent crackle, we could hear the excitement as Arthur Wint thundered past Herb McKenley. Everyone in the White City Stadium started rising to applaud the spectacular finish of the 400 metre race final and we, too, began to jump for joy. Jamaica had gained its first Olympic Gold Medal through an awesome display of skill and grit by a master athlete. In taking the Silver as well, Jamaica had served notice of things yet to come.

Arthur Wint's triumph in 1948 served to etch his name forever in the annals of Olympic lore and planted an irremovable landmark in the journey of our Jamaican people. It was a superb demonstration that Jamaicans could beat the best in the rest of the world and a further spur to those who believed we had the capacity and resolve to proceed in the building of our own Sovereign Nation.

For me, as a young schoolboy then, Wint became an instant idol. By the time I had the privilege of meeting him, Arthur Stanley Wint was already a living legend.

The Longer Run: A Daughter's Story of Arthur Wint reflects much more than the stellar achievements of an outstanding athlete. It reveals his major accomplishments as surgeon, diplomat and community builder. While Valerie Wint admits openly to hero-worshipping her Dad, she does not engage in a jaundiced presentation. The accolades she showers on her father appear well deserved. As one delves through the pages, in addition to his outstanding exploits as an athlete, other qualities are revealed that would establish Wint's right to the pedestal on which he is deservingly placed.

Valerie captures all the drama of the challenges and accomplishments of her legendary father on and off the circuit in this well written book.

Readers are provided with a rare glimpse into the family life of this Caribbean superstar: his long period of courtship with the woman who would eventually become his wife, Norma; the couple's relationship with their three daughters and grandchildren; and the impact of their years of agreed separation on family life.

The book offers more than a glimpse of Norma Wint, who I had come to know during my student days at the Mona Campus. Beneath that quiet disposition, dignified carriage and graceful frame, there was always evident that inner strength which provided enduring support to her husband and the proper nurturing of her children at every stage.

Amazingly, although daughter Valerie was not born until after her father's medal winning exploits on the international circuit, her fly-on-the-wall accounts are engagingly facilitated by seamless quotations of personal experiences from those closest to him at the important times. Openly lavish in her admiration, the intimate details on his disappointments, setbacks and failures serve to avert the pitfalls of undue adulation.

This liberally illustrated and reader-friendly publication covers a slice of Caribbean history related to the 72 years of Arthur Wint's life – outlining his globetrotting and Second World War experiences as a Flight Lieutenant in the RAF, the post war immigration period and life for those who became the vanguard of black settlement in the mother country; the independence and the post independence era; the subsequent period of social unrest in Jamaica; community life in Kingston and Lucea, where he established his practice and spent most of his medical years.

The Longer Run is a compelling social commentary that covers previously existing gaps in our records of Arthur Wint's life as an accomplished public servant, decorated war veteran and diplomat. The work is unsparing in some of its details, a feature that readers will find captivating. There are, however, some surprises in store, including how Wint benefited from the legal acuity of the great Norman Manley, QC, before he went away to join the RAF.

The author tells the story of her father against the political, social and cultural backdrop of the times in which he lived, worked and excelled. We are reminded of the racial prejudice that prevailed in the early years and the far-reaching tentacles of the Cold War. The launch of the Russian satellite Sputnik 1, the assassination of US President John F. Kennedy, the invasion of Grenada and the Walter Rodney riot in Kingston are skilfully interwoven in a fluid story flow.

References to incidents and general developments in Jamaica are many: ranging from disasters such as Hurricane Charlie, the subsequent outbreak of Poliomyelitis in the 1950s, and the Kendal Train Crash. Other key recollections include the memorable visits of Dr Martin Luther King Jr and Emperor Haile Selassie of Ethiopia.

In contextualizing the story, Valerie introduces readers to her mother's colourful kin, the Marshes, a prominent, typically 'brown-skinned' and 'middle class' family. She shares fond memories of life in the big house on Beechwood Avenue where she and her mother lived with the extended Marsh clan while Arthur completed his medical studies in the UK.

Such details provide important clues to the origins of the author's strong sense of family which is revealed in the work, as well as the social environment in which her father's life story unfolded. They also add to the endearing quality of the book as an engaging personal tribute to the world renowned, groundbreaking athlete and dedicated public servant by a beloved daughter.

We thank Valerie most sincerely for enriching our historical narrative by this long-overdue account of the life of an icon, a truly inimitable Jamaican hero.

Most Hon. P. J. Patterson, ON, OCC, PC, QC
Former Prime Minister of Jamaica

Acknowledgements

My deepest gratitude to Norma Wint, Arthur's wife and my mother: for the interviews, her written memoirs, and the casual chats; Rachel Manley, award-winning author and my mentor and taskmaster through the first draft; Jim Borecki, my dear husband; my best friend, greatest support and sounding board; Alison Wint and Colleen Wint-Smith, my sisters: for their memories; Lloyd Wint, Arthur's brother and Mavis Edwards, Arthur's sister: for their reminiscences; Lauren Alexis Bauer, my son and Arthur's grandson, for the mural he created that became the design for the cover; Anna Bauer-Ross, my daughter and Arthur's granddaughter, for her insights into my story; Jean Beaumont, Mavis's daughter, my cousin, who edited our grandfather's memoirs; and Susan White, a journalism teacher, my great friend from university, and also a sounding board.

I am also grateful to the many persons who accommodated me for interviews: Chappie and Jean Marsh, my mother's brother and late sister-in-law; the late Wesley Powell, Founder and former Headmaster of Excelsior School; John Parlett, former member of Polytechnic Harriers Athletics Club and University of London Athletics Club, Arthur's friend and athletic rival; Mike Fennell, Jamaica Olympic Association; Herb McKenley, Arthur's teammate and rival at 400 metres;

Elward Burnside, Aircrew Association, Toronto, Canada; Don Mills, Arthur's friend; Donovan Bailey, Jamaican-Canadian sprinter and motivational speaker, Toronto, Canada; Colin Cooper, Toronto, Canada, a fan of Arthur's as a schoolboy in England; Lois 'Dot' Clarke, Secretary to Arthur at the High Commission in London; the Canadian National Library and Archives, Ottawa, Canada; and the Directorate of History, Canadian Department of National Defence, Ottawa, Canada.

Hero Worship

I hero-worshipped my father. Of that there can be no doubt, certainly more so since his death. Are all daughters like that?

Arthur Wint was famous. Not in the way a movie star is famous, but within Jamaican society in general, and within the athletic community in particular, he was well known and respected. I never really knew this until quite late – in my teens, I guess. He was just Daddy. He worked inordinately long hours, and for many of my formative years he simply wasn't there. It's not as though he took off and left us, it's that his work always took precedence over the family – and I resented that. Come to think of it, I still do.

He was so well known that once I was walking in the small village of Rock Spring, Hanover, when a little elderly man approached me saying, 'You must be Dr Wint's daughter.' I asked how he knew that. 'You walk just like him,' he responded. There was nowhere to hide in Jamaica – one had to be circumspect.

Even living in Canada, many years after my father's passing in 1992, I find that he is still revered. I came to running late in life myself, never having been much of an athlete in my teens. I began at the grand old age of 51 to run long distances, albeit very slowly. Recently as I was running alone one Saturday morning, I came upon a fellow runner and as usual, we greeted each other. We ran in tandem for a while, and chatted about running. Recognising his accent, I asked him where he was from. 'Jamaica,' he said. 'You too?' 'Yes,' I replied. We talked about where in Jamaica we hailed from, and then I said, 'If you're a runner and you're from Jamaica, you probably know who my father was.' He looked at me with a query in his eyes. 'My father was Arthur Wint.' The gentleman stopped dead in his tracks, shook my hand and then hugged me. 'Of course I know who he was. One of the greatest runners ever!' And so we ran on together amicably, sharing our love and respect for Arthur Wint.

Arthur Wint, my father, was Jamaica's first Olympic Gold Medallist. He had been a Flight Lieutenant in the RAF during the Second World War, and went on to become a doctor and surgeon. His medical career was put on hold for four years in the 1970s when he was appointed Jamaica's High Commissioner to the United Kingdom (UK). He was a very public person, instantly recognisable, but at the same time a very private man.

The thing is, I don't believe I ever really knew him. For most of my life he was an absentee father – always present in spirit, but not always present in my day to day life – and so there are layers and depths to him that I will never be able to access. There are crucial aspects to his life that I can only interpret from afar.

It was apparent very early on that Arthur's medical career was the priority. He had dedicated himself to helping others, and this necessarily took him away from us. When I was six, he left Mummy – pregnant with my younger sister Colleen – two-year-old Alison and me, to go to England to study surgery. My mother, sisters and I joined him there when Colleen was a year old. We all lived together for four years in England, and for two or three years after we returned to Jamaica. Then when I was 13, he went to work first in Falmouth, then in Lucea, and I never lived with him again. Alison and Colleen got that opportunity when he was appointed High Commissioner to England in 1973. They had the chance to live with him and know him as teenagers, whereas I only saw him on holidays through all my teen years. I resented this.

As I didn't live with him, my image of him is as other, distant, even exotic. My mother was the one I was with every day, knocking heads, driving each other mad. When my father was around, life was a holiday – literally – as we were with him for weekends and holidays, and we were never alone with him. It wasn't a matter of being 'sent' to our father, or of him having access for two weekends a month. My parents weren't divorced. They weren't even officially separated. They had simply made the decision to live apart so that we could have the benefit of good schools, for which I am grateful, but I do believe it was the wrong decision for their marriage.

My father was tall. In another time he could easily have been a superb basketball player. At 6 feet 5½ inches and very slim, he was always easy to spot in a crowd – or should I say above the crowd. His long legs and arms meant he had to have shirts and pants specially tailored for him. When we lived in England his shirts were made with extra-long tails in the back to cover his rear end and keep it warm in winter. His head was narrow and long, with ears that were on the verge of protruding. When he washed his hair, he would 'set' it by wearing a 'stocking cap' made from one of my mother's cast-off stockings.

Daddy's clothes were, if not unique, then special. In the early 1960s when the TV show 'Doctor Kildare' was popular, my father recognised the practicality of the shirts Kildare wore at work. Consequently, my mother had such shirts made for him. They did not button down the centre of the front in the traditional way, but across the shoulder and down the left side, and were worn without a tie. That way, his shirtfront and tie would not get in his way when examining a patient. So Daddy wore his Doctor Kildare shirts for years, until the day came when men's fashion in Jamaica changed and allowed him to go to work tieless.

He was an inveterate smoker. He always had a cigarette in his long fingers, often with an extremely long ash that would fall onto his trousers. In England, he also smoked a pipe. I really liked the smell of the pipe, and was sorry that he gave it up because of the heat when we moved back to Jamaica. In his later years he made a token effort to quit smoking – he got those cigarette filters that were supposed to progressively wean you off nicotine. They didn't work for him, but yet he continued to use them. The only time he didn't smoke was in the week before his death.

My father was a very special man. From him I learned probably my most valuable lesson – how to be comfortable with both the powerful and the lowly. He grew up the son of a rural Presbyterian minister, so he was intimate with the ways of the people. Yet as a famous athlete, and later as a diplomat, he had to hobnob with those of high rank in society. Somewhere along the way he figured out how to be sociable and respectful with all he met. I remember when he was Jamaica's High Commissioner to the UK, dealing daily with ministers of government and diplomats, his greatest relaxation was to come home to Jamaica, to Negril, and play a raucous game or two of dominoes with the local guys, or to 'knock back two rum' in a little rum bar. My mother would not have been caught dead in a rum bar, but Daddy felt quite at home there.

My father loved music, as does my mother. There was always music around us, either in the background where we absorbed it subconsciously, or in the foreground. Both my parents had beautiful voices, and Daddy from time to time sang in a choir. In fact, he was instrumental in starting the Hanover Parish Choir.

We always sang in the car on long trips – as a child my favourite song was 'Faldaree' or 'The Happy Wanderer' – the one about travelling 'with my knapsack on my back.' This was *my personal* song, because my father changed the words by making 'Faldaree' become 'Valerie.'

As I understand it from some of those who have known him, my father had a bit of an eye for the ladies. He was quite circumspect and these friendships did not interfere with his love and responsibility for his family. I doubt if Mummy ever seriously looked at another man in her life as she was very rigidly bound by duty and a sense of what was right and proper – my own rebellions, and indeed much of my life, have been deeply coloured by her rigidity. Daddy, however, I'm sure, had at least one other serious relationship with a woman, maybe more. I will never know the extent of this friendship with a woman in Lucea where he was working, but he was an attractive, virile man, living, to all intents and purposes alone, and she was an attractive woman. I met her later and she was a very amicable, interesting woman with whom I had a good relationship.

Arthur Wint wasn't one to show his emotions openly. He was a very private man, really, and one tended to see only a small part of the whole man. One thing that is certain is that he took his responsibilities seriously, and thought nothing of helping someone in need. Consequently, he inspired immense loyalty from colleagues and acquaintances, as well as from close friends and family.

Of course, the path he took in life was not chosen with the intention of becoming wealthy. To begin with, he came to medicine relatively late in life, his studies having been interrupted by the War. Consequently, he didn't qualify as a doctor until his 30s, and he was 43 when he qualified as a surgeon. He therefore didn't have as long a career as others. Also, he worked mainly in the public sector, as a Medical Officer of Health who saw a few private patients. This, coupled with the fact that he was a country doctor, meant he was never destined to be rich. Many of his patients were not able to pay him in cash, so he would accept whatever goods or produce they could afford: a stem of bananas, a chicken, a butchered goat. He practised medicine because that was where he saw a need to be filled. He practised medicine because it filled a need in him to honour life, and he practised medicine in Jamaica, because it is a country he loved passionately.

Nevertheless, there was a darkness that overshadowed Arthur's life. As a child and youth, he had always been very playful, very happy-go-lucky. He didn't take life seriously, and his burgeoning athletic career was his only discipline.

At the age of 19, however, an incident would shock this carefree young man out of his complacency, and make him re-evaluate his life. As a result, Arthur Wint made choices that set him on a path of sacrifice and service.

Childhood and Youth

A six-year-old boy waits impatiently every day for his father to come home. He's taller than average, and very thin and wiry, with boundless energy erupting from every pore.

Father arrives on his horse. This is what the boy, Arthur, has been waiting for. Albert, the yard-boy, takes the horse. He picks Arthur up and places him astride the horse, leaping up himself behind the boy. Together they ride off to tie the horse out in the bush.

On this particular afternoon, Albert puts Arthur onto the horse, and then leaves to take care of some other chore. When he returns, horse and boy are both gone. The horse, accustomed to going to the bush, just went off with him. A great panic and search ensues.

Finally Lloyd, Arthur's younger brother, announces, 'The horse gone up to Congo Town with Arthur.' Everyone goes off to look for them. They find Arthur sitting under a naseberry tree, having been ditched by the horse but none the worse for wear, gazing out at the world and wondering what all the fuss was about.

This is an attitude Arthur would take into adulthood. He would sit on the verandah and ponder life, cigarette in hand, cold glass of beer nearby, wondering, 'What the dickens is all the fuss about?'

My father was born in Plowden, Manchester, on May 25, 1920, the second child of Reverend John Wint and his wife Hilda née Smith. My grandparents were dedicated servants of the Presbyterian Church in Jamaica – my grandfather realised his vocation at 19 years old to train for the ministry and this became his life. He was also a son of the soil: his parents owned property in Pike in central Jamaica where they grew and processed coffee and ginger, and farmed other crops and goats. The children were expected to work on the property before and after school. When he became a minister, he spent his life ministering in rural communities similar to those in which he had grown up, and he continued his farming endeavours – he even tried his hand at bee keeping. My grandparents lived through the hardships of two world wars and political upheaval at home in Jamaica, as well as several natural disasters, and through it all their first thought was their people's welfare.

The Wints and their five children – Mavis, Arthur, Lloyd, Douglas and Kathleen – moved often, all over Jamaica, because of my grandfather's occupation. They served in Falmouth, Plowden, Port Maria, Mount Zion and Brownsville. Everywhere they moved Hilda – most often known as 'Mater' – opened a school, and started various youth and women's groups. The Wint children all started school at age five, even though you weren't supposed to do so until age seven. It just made sense – there wasn't anything else for them to do except get into trouble. Consequently, whenever the School Inspector was coming around, the young Wints were hustled out the back door of the school. Of course, the Inspector would be coming to the home of the schoolmistress for lunch, and the schoolmistress was their own mother. This was a big secret that everyone knew about, and the wise Inspector said nothing.

Later, when Arthur was about nine years old and they were living in Port Maria, St Mary, he 'fell in love' with a girl in his big sister Mavis's class. He decided to tell her of his feelings by writing her a letter.

Unsure about his spelling, he showed the letter to his mother. To his chagrin, she thoroughly dissected this missive, critiquing not only his spelling, but also his grammar and sentence structure. The final blow came when she said, 'One more thing. Never use crayon to write a note to a girl. Now go and write it out properly.'

'Needless to say,' Arthur said, 'I was devastated, and I never pursued the young lady in question again.'

By the time Arthur was 11, he was boarding at Calabar High School in Kingston, and soon became one of the school's star athletes. Arthur got his first pair of spikes when he was about 11 or 12. Lloyd recounts,

> It was a thick, heavy pair of pigskin, and he was so glad to get the pair of spikes, man, the day before Championships he's there jumping up and down in the dormitory. It was just the one shoe he had on, not two, and he stuck the spike right through his big toenail. And he ran with it!

He most likely won his race too!

Lloyd also tells the story that at about the same age, Arthur was running in an under-13 race.

> In those days, the boys wore shorts with a hole in the front. Arthur was ahead, and as he came round

the bend to the tape, his little tommy jumped out!
There was it wagging in front of him. And he
wouldn't stop. He ran with it right through the
tape, but he never stopped, he went past before he
adjusted himself.

The brothers hero-worshipped Arthur. He was a
natural athlete – 'There was nothing Arthur couldn't do,
as far as we were concerned,' says Lloyd. In a district sports
meeting in Galina, Port Maria, Arthur beat all the grown
men in a 220-yard race at the age of 14.

I don't know if you knew, but your father was a
swimmer. He has medals in swimming. He got as
far as the quarter or semi-finals in tennis – in those
days they used to have under-16 junior tennis
championships – but he never had any particular
training in tennis. I think he was wicket keeper
for second eleven cricket, and kept goal for second
eleven football. You name it, he did it.

Arthur's life at Calabar was centred on athletics. He
gained the nickname 'Bumpy' that followed him throughout
his life, because of his colourful description in a botany
class, of a soursop – 'It bumpy-bumpy and gritty-gritty all
over.' Yet he paid scant attention to his academics, and as
a result, failed his Junior Matriculation exams. Reverend
Price the Headmaster – known familiarly as 'Old Price' –
told him in no uncertain terms that he was not going to get
ahead in life based solely on the 'talent in his feet.'

So at the age of about 16, as Arthur tells it, he
immediately got in touch with his father, asking to be
removed from Calabar. His older sister Mavis says she was
the one who alerted their father:

> I felt he wouldn't settle down to do work. I said
> to him, 'You think athletics is going to take you
> through life?' As a matter of fact his headmaster
> told him, 'Young Wint carries his brains in his feet.'
> I wasn't satisfied with his performance at Calabar,
> because after all these years, all he was doing was
> running. So when I was in Kingston now I wrote
> Dad and told him he must send him to Excelsior,
> because it was a new school and would be good for
> Arthur.

Regardless of who initiated it, Arthur was moved to this new private school, Excelsior, which had been started only a few years earlier in 1931. He felt there was nothing more that Calabar had to offer him. Reverend Wint, knowing his son, and annoyed that he had failed his exams, made the journey to Kingston. The two went to Excelsior to see its founder and Principal, Wesley Powell. It was 1937. Arthur was to remain at Excelsior for about two years, two very crucial years of his life.

This interview was the start of a new and exciting chapter in Arthur's life. Reverend Price, according to Powell, heard about this interview and wrote to Powell, saying that it would be doing my father a disservice to remove him from Calabar with its strong athletics programme to this new private school with no playing fields. Excelsior School focused on academics, and students had to go to Race Course nearby (where National Heroes Circle is now situated) for any athletics.

After Powell received Price's letter, he contacted Arthur's father and asked what he would like to do. Reverend Wint was clearly impressed with what he saw at this new school, because he came back to Excelsior and registered not only Arthur, but also Lloyd and Douglas, who were also attending Calabar. They boarded at the school – the original school was at 18 North Street, with the boarders staying next door at number 16.

Excelsior was still a very young school and small enough that Mr Powell could give students special attention and individual coaching. He says,

> I found Arthur very receptive and I undertook to coach him individually. We entered him for the Senior Cambridge Exam, as it was then. He had failed Junior at Calabar, and his father was quite disgusted. He passed with an ordinary pass and I induced him to re-sit the examination and then he passed with exemptions from London Matriculation, and this is what stood him in good stead later when he wanted to study medicine.

Arthur had done so well in the Cambridge exams that Powell would later offer him a teaching post as sports master. Arthur helped Excelsior rise in the rankings of private secondary school sports, while his two brothers Lloyd and Douglas, strong athletes in their own right, also helped in this athletic development.

Despite the lack of proper training facilities at Excelsior, Arthur continued to pursue his athletics under the coaching of Sir Herbert MacDonald. In February 1938, at the age of 17, Arthur was part of the Jamaican contingent to the Fourth Central American Games in Panama. During those Games, he ran the 800 metres in 1:56.3, winning Gold and creating a new Central American record. He also won Bronze in the 400-metre hurdles. Herb McKenley, who was a younger boy at Calabar, and who would later be Arthur's Olympic teammate, recalls,

> He came to Calabar dressed in the Jamaica uniform, which was a cream suit, with white shirt, maroon tie, white shoes, white socks, and a Panama hat – what we would call a Jippi-Jappa hat. As you know, he was very tall and slim, and of course he came there for us to see him. I was so impressed! The only way I can describe it is to say he looked regal. I said quietly to myself, 'One day I must wear that uniform.'

It was at Excelsior that Arthur met Norma Dorothea Marsh. She and her brother Chappie were also students there – her brother Derry was to follow later – and she was enrolled in the Commercial department. Arthur was so smitten with this beautiful, leggy young woman that he also enrolled in Commercial, so as to be near her. Norma had, of course, already heard of Arthur Wint because of his athletics, and in particular because of his exploits in Panama.

Clearly the attraction was mutual. Norma was smitten, and so she and Arthur, his two brothers and her two brothers became fast friends. They would gather at the Marsh home, and the boys would get up to pranks. According to Lloyd, one day the Wint brothers were with the Marshes, when all of a sudden Arthur exclaimed, 'Good God, you know I'm supposed to be running at Sabina Park!' Everyone piled into my grandfather BC's car and headed for Sabina Park. When they arrived, coach Herbert MacDonald said to him, 'Wint, you're too late. What happened to you?' He replied, 'I completely forgot about it, Mr Mac. But is there anything else I can enter?' MacDonald told him that the only entry that was not closed was the long jump. He entered the event and jumped 24 feet and a half-inch, thus setting a new Jamaican record.

As Lloyd puts, it,

> Norma and Arthur were together from school days. Always. No matter what happened wherever they went they were always together. They always kept in touch. And when we were in London, if Arthur was going away running, he would say, 'You look after Norma till I come back.' I would take her to pictures, or go out with her somewhere to eat. But it's been like that from school days.

Arthur Wint was beginning to come into his own academically and socially, and was well on his way to becoming a national track hero. The world, however, was on the brink of war, and Arthur would soon put his athletic ambitions on hold so he could play his small part in that global cataclysm.

Norma and Arthur
A Love Story

By the time a child is old enough to separate themselves from their parents, and to see them as human beings in their own right with an emotional life, very often the parents are into their middle or even later years. The child, now a young adult, has great difficulty in imagining the parents as children themselves, much less falling in love and experiencing the heady emotions and physical sensations that go along with new love.

So it was with my parents and me. They came into my consciousness as a unit already formed. As I went through the teen years and the angst and rebellion those entailed, I was convinced that they could not possibly understand anything I was going through, because of course they had never experienced anything similar. It wasn't until I was a young mother myself that I started to see them in a different light. Naturally they had lived full lives before I came along, they had met and fallen in love as teenagers, but were separated by war for many years. It speaks to the strength of their original relationship that they were able to eventually come together and create the unit that became known as 'Arthur and Norma.'

Norma Dorothea was the eldest child and only daughter of BC Marsh and Ena 'S'Ene' McBean. Born in

1921 in Kingston, Norma was an urban child who lived in her grandmother's house downtown near the harbour. As her mother S'Ene (a contraction of 'Miss Ena') was still a teenager when Norma was born, Grandma McBean was the adult in the home. Her father BC was somewhat older than S'Ene, and he was from the parish of St Mary, in northeastern Jamaica.

Kingston, Jamaica in the 1930s was still very much a colonial town, where white residents had the privileges, and those who had African blood were lower down the scale, depending on how much African was visible – the lighter the skin was, the more privileges one had. Consequently, even within a family where one child was lighter-skinned than a sibling, that child would have greater opportunities in life.

Despite the fact that people were often held back because of their skin colour, this was not so in my mother's family. The Marshes were 'brown-skinned' and so her father was able to work in the Civil Service. His name was Burford Clayton, but everyone called him 'BC'. He had a great love of the law and would go to the law courts to listen to the cases – in particular he enjoyed listening to the successes of Norman Manley, who was in his heyday then. When BC came home from these forays he would arrange a 'kangaroo court' in the backyard and have the case re-enacted with the children and their friends. No doubt it was this early exposure that led to both Marsh boys becoming lawyers, and later judges, in their own right.

S'Ene's mother, my great-grandmother, Elizabeth McBean was a very strong influence in all our lives. She was part Scottish, and therefore quite light-skinned, and as a result was able to work at the prestigious Myrtle Bank Hotel in Kingston. She eventually left that job to look after the house and children, and sewed for other people. She also crocheted beautifully – I remember some of her pieces that graced our tables. As S'Ene was so young when she had her children – they are quite close together in age – Grandma McBean helped to raise them. All the children's friends came to call her Grandma.

Norma and her two brothers have always been very close. She is the eldest, but Chappie and then Derry followed quickly after. It is my mother who coined the nickname 'Chappie.' When he was born, Grandma McBean looked at this baby and commented that he had big feet 'like Charlie Chaplin.' My mother, who was three then, heard this and called him Chappie, and the name stuck. His given names are Owen Dustin, but no one ever calls him that. Derry, a little more than a year younger than Chappie, came by his name in a more legitimate way, in that his given name is Waldo Dermot.

Even from childhood, Chappie was always the quieter, more introspective brother. A Libra, he demonstrated the balance that his Zodiac sign epitomises: on the one hand he was an academic – he became a lawyer, and was always reading and learning and delving into how things worked; on the other hand, he loved to build and mend and fix things. Uncle Chappie was always there, even when my father left to study in England. He built me a swing set and a sandbox under the Julie mango tree, where I spent long hours creating worlds of my own. He also taught me to wield a hammer, a plane, a saw and a screwdriver – any handy skills I may have are entirely due to his influence.

When I was seven years old he decided to build flagstones for the walkway and I was his helper, pouring cement and mixing sand and water in the correct consistency. In later years, whenever anything needed fixing, the first person to call was Uncle Chappie.

Derry was the more flamboyant brother. According to my mother, he was somewhat of a rebel, and constantly in trouble. Like my father and his brothers, Derry joined the RAF and trained as a pilot in Canada, and was later stationed in England. For him the glamour of being an RAF pilot was exhilarating, and the experiences and the sense of camaraderie stayed with him throughout his life. He too became a lawyer and eventually a judge, and as long as I knew him he would always be the devil's advocate in any arguments. Derry was also quite a wit, given to making puns that would cause all around him to groan. One of these puns that I remember from my childhood was actually a bilingual one: he would end his stories with the phrase 'Hacienda my story.' I picked up on this and, not getting the joke really, once ended a school essay with that phrase. To this day I wonder what the teacher thought! As Derry grew older, his devil's advocacy grew stronger, to the point where young friends of my generation would call him 'Judge Dredd' after a popular movie and song character.

Education was a most important part of the Marsh family life. After completing elementary school, Norma was sent to a small private school where she prepared for and won a scholarship to St Andrew High School for Girls in Kingston. The school was founded in 1925, and my mother was one of its early students. She developed a love of reading very early, and was constantly immersed in a book. On holidays in St Mary, when the boys were learning how to ride horses, she would escape into her literature. She tells me that she would climb a particular tree in her yard where she was able to read her *Elsie Dinsmore* or *What Katy Did* books undisturbed. She remained an avid reader until well into her 80s, and passed on her love of the written word to me.

Norma left St Andrew's and went to pursue commercial studies at Excelsior School in the late 1930s, where she would meet Arthur Wint later on. He was tall, handsome, and had already gained recognition as an athlete from his successes in Boys' Championships representing Calabar High School, and from his gold-medal performance at the 1938 Central American Games in Panama. Norma had heard about him while she was still in the sixth form (Grade 13) at St Andrew High School for Girls.

She writes in her memoirs:

> In February of that year we sixth formers were pleased to learn that our athletes had distinguished themselves at the Pan American Games. A paper of that time *The Jamaica Standard* had a graphic account by the coach G.C. Foster how Arthur Wint had beaten the odds and won a brilliant race at the Games. He predicted he would be a world-beater.
>
> 'Who is this Wint anyway?' I asked another sixth former.
>
> 'He's a long foot bwoy who goes to Calabar' she replied.

In January 1939 I went to Excelsior College to be trained in commercial subjects for the working world. On certain days sixth form boys from the school would come to our section to join the bookkeeping class. They were in a different class across the room, but I felt someone gazing at me and I looked up and caught the eye of a young man. We gazed at each other for what seemed a long time.

Later I learned that this was Wint, the 'long foot bwoy' who had come from Calabar College.

The two started talking casually, as fellow students. The school would occasionally have concerts, and Norma took part in these with her lovely singing voice. Arthur now lent his strong baritone to the shows as well. Norma also took note of how well Arthur organised the school's track meets, showing his leadership and motivational skills, as he encouraged the other students to get involved.

Norma was strongly attracted to Arthur, but in the true teenage fashion of the day she was reticent about letting him know how she felt. However, her friend Dulcie eventually pulled off a ruse by phoning Arthur and then putting the two of them on the phone together. So Norma and Arthur started seeing each other. They would go dancing at Springfield Club on Windward Road in a group with other friends, including Norma's brothers. They also went on hikes and to the Saturday matinee movies at the new Carib Theatre in Cross Roads. After getting to know each other for a while, Arthur very formally asked her father's permission to go out with Norma, which was the turning point of their relationship. After this, Norma and Arthur were always together, as Lloyd puts it, and any other potential suitors backed off. BC and S'Ene accepted Arthur, and he became great friends with Grandma McBean.

Norma's father BC loved to watch his daughter dance with Arthur, particularly to the 'Blue Danube Waltz.' BC had a club foot (*Talipes Equinovarus* or *Diles Smith Syndrome*) and so was unable to dance himself, but was impressed by how agile Arthur was for such a long, gangly young man. The couple would attend many private house parties as well as the dance clubs, where they enjoyed dancing with each other. In those days, Norma says, they didn't have sex, as teens tend to do these days. 'We would hug and kiss, and there was feeling and touching, but no sex as such. We took part in various teenage pursuits, usually in a group.'

My mother is quite light-skinned, while my father was dark. Given the prejudices of the day, I wondered whether her parents might have had misgivings about her going out with a man so much darker than she. My mother maintains that her parents never discussed colour, and that they had friends of all shades and races coming and going at their home. Her parents never expressed any misgivings, not to her at least. However, she learned later that BC did in fact harbour these thoughts, as he told Gladys, one of his cousins, that 'Norma is not to marry any black man.' Arthur was such a charming man though, one with such charisma and potential, that Norma's parents could not help but take to him.

After my mother completed her commercial studies at Excelsior School in the late 1930s, she went to work for the Government in the Treasury Department. Her income helped to pay for her brothers to attend that same school so they could get the opportunity to study in England. By so doing, Norma gave up her chances at university herself, one of many sacrifices she would make for her brothers, her husband, and for us, her children. All her close girlfriends ultimately went to university and became professional women – a judge, a couple of university professors, a social welfare worker – and I've often wondered if she felt bitter about the sacrifice she had to make for her brothers. She maintains that she has no regrets, so perhaps I am projecting my own feelings.

While my parents were at Excelsior, a precarious political situation in Jamaica escalated, from the 1938 workers' riots, building up to a strong nationalist movement. Outside Jamaica, tensions were escalating in Europe – Hitler had invaded Poland on September 1, 1939, and two days later England declared war on Germany. England at war meant Jamaica was at war, but for an 18-year-old and 19-year-old just beginning to discover each other, and struggling with the demands of school and exams, the War must have seemed very far away. However, as the War progressed, and as Norma and Arthur became more aware of what was going on, they became increasingly conscious of the need for action: they both felt they must do something to help England, and to take part in this most important event of their lifetime.

Consequently, in autumn 1942, after completing his matriculation and starting to work in the Civil Service, Arthur enlisted in the RAF and left Jamaica for training in Canada. In true Arthur form, he made all the arrangements and then told Norma – presenting her with a fait accompli, something he would do throughout their lives. The details of his departure were quite hush-hush, as he was not allowed to divulge these arrangements due to wartime secrecy.

A year later, against her parents' wishes, Norma enlisted in the ATS (Auxiliary Territorial Services) and left on the New Zealand merchant ship *Rimutaka* in convoy with military ships. BC and S'Ene were concerned about how their only daughter would fare in England, with not only the War to contend with, but also the inhospitable weather and colour prejudice they anticipated. As it turned out, Norma was never to see her father again.

First, however, before he had entertained any thoughts of participating in the War, in early 1941 something would happen to Arthur that would forever change his life.

The Incident

It was January 1941, and Arthur was not yet 21 years old. He had left Excelsior, having been successful in the various matriculation examinations, and was working for the Jamaican Government's Civil Service as an assistant in the Titles Office. He was young, carefree, and becoming well known as an athlete in Jamaica – just the previous September he had garnered several trophies and was named champion athlete at a Jamaica Amateur Athletics Association (JAAA) meet in Kingston.

One day in mid-January Arthur went into the office vault for some documents he needed and saw the cashier's gun lying there. The office messenger Ida Forbes happened to be in the vault at the same time. Now Arthur had a reputation for being playful – skylarking, as his brother puts it – so it was in this vein that he looked at the young woman, pointed the gun and said, 'I bet you I shoot you.' In the same playful spirit, Forbes held up her hands. Arthur pulled the trigger. Forbes died instantly. Arthur had no knowledge about guns. He hadn't known that the safety catch was not on. He didn't know it was loaded.

His elder sister Mavis tells the story:

> When we asked him what happened, or how it happened, he just said, 'Well we had the gun the day before and it didn't have any bullets in it.'

That's what he said to me. He just thought it was like that, that it didn't have any bullets in it and he just took it up and thought he would tease her with it.

Wesley Powell, his headmaster from Excelsior recounts that he was one of the first of Arthur's supporters to step up and start taking charge of the situation.

Instead of going down to Arthur, first I went to Norman Manley, because I know there was big trouble in it. Sure enough, my friend Norman sympathized with the whole thing. He never charged a cent, and Arthur was relieved in the preliminary enquiries.

Manley represented him and got him two years' probation, which fortunately did not prevent him from joining the Air Force later. Due to his athletic association, his coach Herbert MacDonald also came to the rescue. When Arthur was released on bail, MacDonald wouldn't let him go back to the place where he was living at the time. He took Arthur home, and kept him through that whole period of his trial.

During the trial, several members of the staff from the Titles Office were called to testify. According to the *Daily Gleaner* newspaper, one such witness remembered being in the lunchroom when he saw Forbes pass by in the direction of the office. Not long after that, he heard what sounded like an explosion coming from the strongroom. He went in that direction and before reaching the strongroom Wint ran out and said to him, 'My God, Tommy what am I to do? Up to yesterday I had the gun and it was empty.' This witness pointed out that on several occasions he too had seen the gun and had never seen it loaded.

Mr Norman Manley, KC, represented my father, and in his summation – as described in the *Daily Gleaner* – he requested that the original plea of 'not guilty' be changed to 'guilty.' However, he pleaded for leniency in the sentencing:

> But on final consideration, it seemed more consistent with what I know to be the deep and profound regret and penitence of Wint for this tragic happening that he should make the plea he has made [guilty] and leave to Your Honour to do what seems right….Wint, Your Honour, is a young man. He is only 21 years old. He is the son of very esteemed parents….He was attending Secondary Schools and ended up at Excelsior College, and has recently been in the Government Service as an assistant….I am informed by his Headmaster, and it perhaps throws some light on what happened in this case, that he is indeed very young for his years. He is very playful and always ready to make some joke with everyone that he meets….I ask Your Honour to look upon it as a tragedy that cannot be paid for, and to note that this young man has deeply regretted and sorrowed over it. I feel, in his case, Your Honour may be asked to exercise the highest prerogative of mercy you can under the circumstances.

In his sentencing address to my father, Mr Justice Carberry spoke of his

> …folly and stupidity, folly which a man of your years should not have manifested – your folly on this occasion will no doubt cast a gloom over your whole life. It will affect and make you feel

> uncomfortable for a considerable time....I feel
> that the justice of the case – that all the facts, the
> impression which this case has made on you, and
> the regret and penitence which you feel – that
> these facts and this penitence carry with them the
> punishment you deserve....But while I hope that
> the facts of this case will not lead to melancholia
> and will not affect you adversely, I hope that your
> experience will steady you in life and help in
> shaping your manhood (*Daily Gleaner*, April 29,
> 1941).

Not much is said about the unfortunate woman who
lost her life at the hands of this careless young man. There
is no mention as to whether she left children behind – she
was 30 years old, so there may have been a family. In the
article on her memorial service, the *Daily Gleaner* does
indicate that she had been for many years a member of
St Mark's Church on West Street, and a member of the
church choir. I can only surmise how her death was received
by her loved ones and friends, and I have to speculate that
their feelings might have been bitter as my father became
increasingly famous and his name the stuff of newspaper
headlines.

Following the incident, Wesley Powell offered him
a teaching post as sports master at Excelsior. 'While he
was around,' says Powell, 'we became prominent in private
secondary school sports, and there are no two ways about
it. Arthur, as well as the two brothers Lloyd and Douglas,
who followed in his footsteps. They carried the Excelsior
flag, and made the school prominent on the athletic field.'
In July 1941, just two months after sentencing, my father
would participate in a major international athletic meet at

Sabina Park, and break his own Jamaican record for long jump. No doubt his strict training regimen saved him from the possibility of melancholy and depression.

A year and a half later, in fall 1942, Arthur enlisted in the RAF and left Jamaica for flight training in Canada, and did not return until he had completed his medical studies and had won Olympic Gold.

I never knew about this unfortunate turn of events until after my father's death, and then only because one of my father's old friends and a one-time athletic rival said to me at a wedding, 'It's a pity what happened to him, though.' When I asked for more, this man merely referred me to my uncle. It was never talked about in our home. However, I did go to my uncle and learned more, and once I knew of the circumstances, much of my father's drive and determination and mystery became much clearer to me.

It is my deep feeling that this tragic episode made a huge difference in Arthur's life. It certainly had a sobering effect on a very playful young man – Justice Carberry called it correctly. However, he did not sink into melancholy, but rose from these depths to great heights. As he moved through the various stages of his life – as an RAF pilot and officer, as an athlete and elder statesman of his track team, as a doctor and surgeon, as a diplomat – I believe he was constantly trying to make up for having taken somebody's life. I think this incident informed the choices he would make throughout the rest of his life, and helped to mould the man he would become.

War Years

The cataclysm that was the Second World War (1939–45) was to be a pivotal element in the lives of both Arthur and Norma, as well as many of their friends and relatives. It brought out their sense of duty and longing for excitement, inciting them to action by joining the war in various ways, and ultimately defining who they were to be in their later years.

My father was 19 when the Second World War began in 1939, the same year he met Norma Marsh. He had travelled to Panama the year before, where he had done well in the Central American Games, and was somewhat of a celebrity at home. Jamaica was still in the throes of the political and social upheaval that had come to a head in 1938, and so political awareness was high and a desire to be involved was strong.

Jamaicans had been instilled with very strong connections to the 'Mother Country' – ironic, as the vast majority of Jamaicans are of African slave heritage and so have little for which to thank Britain. However, the brown middle class, this growing intelligentsia, and of course the lighter-skinned upper class, were deeply influenced by all things British. They looked to Britain for its sense of culture: there was nothing in Jamaica, they would argue, that could be as good as what could be acquired in Britain

– no art, no literature, no music, no history. Nothing that was produced in Jamaica, by Jamaicans, could possibly have any value, except the sugar, rum and bananas through which the colonisers' fortunes were made. There was very much an attitude of 'God Save the King,' and 'God Save the British Empire.'

At the onset of the War, a state of emergency was declared in Jamaica under Wartime Emergency Regulations. As a Crown Colony, Jamaica was actually part of Britain, therefore if Britain was at war, so was Jamaica. The daily newspapers and the newsreels at the cinemas were full of war updates and analyses. Adolph Hitler's Germany was threatening the security of England and, by extension, Jamaica.

The Declaration of War brought rationing of food and fuel, so the effects were felt very close to home. This caused Jamaicans, as they are so adept at doing, to 'tun han' mek fashin' (be inventive). They were called upon to do their part in the War effort. 'Even Mum was knitting socks for the soldiers. As soon as she finished one pair she started another,' says Lloyd, my father's brother.

The *Daily Gleaner* newspaper, in addition to reporting on the War, also established a fund, the 'Bombers for Britain Fund,' to which Jamaicans and concerned folk from other colonies donated. Little Jamaica subsequently raised enough money to buy 12 Blenheim aircraft by 1941, which were donated to Britain. In gratitude for this donation, the RAF's No. 139 Squadron was renamed the No. 139 (Jamaica) Squadron.

In August 1940, Hitler's Luftwaffe began a major offensive on Britain, in what came to be called the 'Battle of Britain.' In early September, the German focus moved to London, the beginning of the 'Blitz,' during which London was attacked on 57 consecutive nights between September 7 and November 2. The heavy raids continued, with further attacks on various British cities through to spring 1941 and beyond. Germany attacked Britain's airfields, ports, radar stations and aircraft factories. The goal was a full-scale invasion of England, but the RAF fiercely challenged the Luftwaffe and they were ultimately forced to withdraw and regroup.

These events were far from home, far from the day to day existence of most Jamaicans, but it lit a fire in their hearts – no less so in my father's. Adding fuel to this fire, were several situations that brought the War right to their front door: the establishment of the Gibraltar Camp for refugees; the establishment of an internment facility at Up Park Camp for prisoners of war, guarded for some time by Canadian and British soldiers; and the continuing social and political upheaval at home that had started in 1938. Through all of this, the young Arthur struggled to find himself.

In 1940 the Gibraltar Camp for refugees was established on the Mona Estate, the site that eventually became the University of the West Indies. Nestled in the long, narrow apex of the triangle-shaped Liguanea Plain, between Long Mountain, Dallas Mountain and the Blue Mountains, Mona Estate was a haven for young boys during the mango season. My father, his brothers and my mother's brothers would borrow my grandfather's car and go to Mona to pick mangos during their years at Excelsior School – they knew this place well. Part of the Mona

Estate would later become a housing development called Mona Heights, where all the Marsh siblings eventually made their homes. To this day, one of the original Mona Estate Bombay mango trees still bear exquisite fruit at my Uncle Chappie's home.

Gibraltar Camp was a facility initially for evacuees from Gibraltar and Malta, and later refugees from other countries, including Spain, Poland, the Netherlands and Finland, as well as a contingent of European Jews. When the Gibraltarian evacuees arrived, Jamaicans lined the roads to greet them, singing 'Welcome Gibraltar,' composed in their honour. There was direct contact between the camp population and the locals, as Jamaicans were employed in the camp initially; there was a police station with Jamaican personnel; and local military bands entertained them. With permission, the evacuees could leave the camp – in fact, some of the women did their shopping in the Papine Market just outside the gate of the camp, and actually went to tell their acquaintances goodbye when they left Jamaica in 1944.

In addition to the evacuee facility, there was also an internment camp on the site of today's Up Park Camp, for prisoners of war – German and Italian nationals originally from West Africa where they had been working as trades people when war broke out. This was similar to the internment camps for Japanese Americans and Canadians. A contingent of Canadian soldiers from Winnipeg was deployed to Jamaica for a year, where they performed guard duty at the POW camp.

One famous internee was in fact not of German nor Italian nationality: the fiery labour activist Alexander

Bustamante, who had risen to prominence during the 1938 political action, was seen to be a threat to the War effort because of his continued activism on behalf of Jamaica's workers. As a result, Jamaica's Governor Sir Arthur Richards ordered that he be interned at Up Park Camp under the Defence of the Realm Act. He remained there from September 1940 until February 1942, during which time there were numerous protest marches and strikes by the workers. Incidentally, war notwithstanding, the political awakening of the Jamaican people continued, as Bustamante formed the Jamaica Labour Party in 1943, and defeated Norman Manley's People's National Party in the country's first general election in 1944.

In addition to the internment and evacuation camps, Jamaicans witnessed American forces in the country, following the US declaration of war with Japan in December 1941 – Jamaica was seen as a strategic point in the Caribbean chain of islands. There were also news reports of US activity elsewhere in the region, as the US hastily built bases to protect the Panama Canal, the oilfields of the Gulf of Mexico, and approaches to the US. Of particular interest to Jamaicans was the construction of the US garrison in Trinidad:

> The construction of these camps, naval bases and airfields was a fast project.…Thousands of workers, black and white, Negro and East Indian, had to clear huge areas before construction crews could do their work. At the same time, down at the harbour of Port of Spain, thousands more workers had to build a vast naval base for seaplanes and enlarge the berth for ships. When it is all finished, there will still be about fifteen or twenty thousand American

soldiers stationed there to garrison this powerful fortress that guards the southern approaches to the Caribbean Sea (Caribbean Wars Untold, Humphrey Metzgen and John Graham).

With evidence of the War in their own backyards, with news of the German attacks on Britain and of the success of the Royal Air Force in repelling them, Jamaican young men and women were stirred to action. Visions of honour, valour and heroism danced in their heads, and many enlisted in the British Army, the Merchant Navy and in the RAF. As my mother puts it, 'The War was the greatest drama in the world, and we wanted to be part of it.'

Embedded in that drama, my father's life continued. He finished high school and went to work at the Government Treasury. He met and fell in love with Norma Marsh. He competed in athletics events. He was a typical, happy-go-lucky young man in many respects, albeit one with an extraordinary athletic gift, but I think that the huge blunder that took a woman's life, threw his own into turmoil. Thanks to the kind attentions of the adults in his life, this blunder would not stop him from living the rest of his life well, but for the moment he had lost his focus. As my mother puts it, 'His life was awry.' The War saved him. It set him on his feet again, and brought out the quiet leadership that would epitomise his future life, and which would earn him the epithet 'The Gentle Giant.'

And so it was that two years after the London Blitz, a year and a half after the tragic accident, he signed up to join the British Commonwealth Air Training Plan (BCATP), and left for air force training in Canada in September 1942.

I've often wondered why he chose the air force rather than the army, which might have been an easier route. The fact is that he was just 22 years old and somewhat restless. He had already tasted fame through his running, had tasted notoriety through the shooting incident, and he was in search of his identity. He wanted something that would feed his sense of adventure, something that would let him excel and not just be one of the crowd, and most important, that would allow him to rise above the stain on his reputation. Flying would appeal at all levels, not least of which is that being a 'flyboy' was very glamorous and prestigious. My uncle also feels that the possibility of scholarships and future educational opportunities might have coloured his decision.

Arthur's two brothers, Lloyd and Douglas, as well as my mother's brother Derry and several other good friends, also joined the RAF, travelling to Canada for training with the BCATP. Derry, the youngest of the group, never saw active duty, but Lloyd and Douglas both saw service in England: Douglas as a navigator and Lloyd as a Flight Sergeant with Bomber Command.

The BCATP was created by the British Government at the start of the Second World War in 1940 and was located in Canada. The majority of recruits came from the Commonwealth countries that were signatories to the Plan – Britain, Canada, Australia and New Zealand – and the aim was to train up to 50,000 aircrew each year. Canada was selected as the best location for this massive initiative, because it had vast spaces and ample supplies of fuel, was far from the theatre of war and so was not susceptible to enemy attack, and Canada had the ability to produce trainer aircraft, spare parts and supplies. In addition to drawing young men from Canada, Australia, and New Zealand, the Plan also trained aircrew from occupied France and Norway, and other parts of the Commonwealth including the British West Indies. These young men were trained in the various skills – pilots, navigators, bombers, ground crew – required by the Royal Air Force (RAF), as well as the Royal Canadian Air Force, and the air forces of Australia and New Zealand. They went to Canada for training on about 230 air bases across the country: my father spent most of 1942, 1943, and some of 1944 on bases in Brandon, Manitoba, as well as locations in Saskatchewan, Ontario and Quebec.

The BCATP website describes the young recruits:

> They are between 18 and 24 years of age. A majority is not yet 20. They chose the Air Force over the Navy and the Army. Most of them share a dream: they picture themselves soaring through the skies on mighty planes, engaging the Fuehrer's minions in mortal combat. The BCATP's task is to direct those rookies towards a training that matches their skills, to provide discipline without hampering their resolution, to impart the know-how needed to conduct dangerous flight missions, to teach the reflexes that may save their lives and the lives of their crewmates.

Arthur made the long voyage from his homeland Jamaica to Halifax on the east coast of Canada, then by train he travelled through New Brunswick and on to Montreal, where he was inducted into the Royal Air Force and given his initial training – air force boot camp, if you will.

Potential pilots and other crew began their training at one of the five Manning Depots, located in Toronto, Brandon, Edmonton, Quebec City and Lachine. There, recruits were taught military discipline and the basics of aviation: regulations, history, and navigation. Between courses they went through endless drills and weapon-handling exercises. Arthur went to the Manning Depot in Lachine, Quebec. From the Manning Depots they were sent to Initial Training School (ITS) for a ten-week programme, wishing and hoping that at the end they would be selected for pilot training, the most prestigious of the many jobs in the Air Force.

Following ITS, those selected to train as pilots underwent a gruelling elementary programme (Elementary Flight Training School) of eight weeks, including about 50 hours' flying time in de Havilland Tiger Moths, Fleet Finches, and Fairchild Cornells. Following this initial training, they progressed to Service Flying Training Schools for 10–16 weeks, where they trained on single-engine North American Harvards, Avro Ansons, Cessna Cranes, and Airspeed Oxfords.

By the time Arthur had completed initial training it was winter, and he was on a train again across this enormous country to Davidson, Saskatchewan, northwest of Regina, about halfway to Saskatoon. Canada is a strange and often daunting place for a young man from the tropics. No one coming from Jamaica is ever prepared for the severity of winter, especially in Manitoba or Saskatchewan, where one can get frostbite just going from one building to another. The temperature can get so cold that your tears can freeze on your face if you're outside for too long. Still Arthur took it all in stride choosing not to fight the elements, but to embrace his new environment – the natural athlete that he was, he even participated in the quintessential Canadian sport of ice hockey, donning skates and learning to skate on the flooded, frozen fields.

When Arthur left Jamaica, he took his running spikes with him – as Lloyd says, he never went anywhere without them. A little inconvenience called War would not prevent him from following his passion. During his two years in Canada, he took part in athletics competitions on the various bases, but perhaps the most significant was on Labour Day, September 6, 1943, an inter-unit track meet that was held at the exhibition grounds in Brandon, Manitoba. My father had just finished his elementary flying training in Davidson, Saskatchewan, and had been posted to the No. 12 Senior Flight Training School in Brandon. He arrived on Saturday, September 4, just in time to enter the track meet. He was one of two outstanding track and field athletes who carried the No. 12 SFTS to victory that day – Sgt Fred Hair of Orillia, Ontario was the other star. The *Brandon Daily Sun* describes the performances:

> A two-man team comprised of Sgt Fred Hair and LAC [Leading Aircraftman] Arthur Wint piled up 32 points in two brilliant individual performances Monday afternoon and it swept No. 12 SFTS to a district services championship in the annual track and field meet held at the Exhibition Grounds... Wint proved a real sensation, as the 6ft. 5in. coloured boy [sic] from Kingston, Jamaica turned in three straight wins in the 440 yards, the broad jump and the hop, step and jump....The Jamaican-born airman came from Dafoe over the

> weekend, and he admitted that this was his first
> athletic competition of the season. But the manner
> in which he ran away from his field in the quarter-
> mile, and in which he travelled the distance in 48
> and 4.5 seconds was one of the highlights of the
> day. Long striding and with perfect rhythm, Wint
> raced as if he was shot out of the gun and he was
> yards ahead at the finish. Then he came back to go
> over 20 feet in the broad jump…which he likewise
> took with ease.

When I imagine my father on one of the flight training stations in Canada, I imagine him in winter and being cold. In addition to his flight suit he would likely have worn long underwear, maybe doubling up on socks and gloves, because not only would it be cold on the ground, but up in the planes it must also have been incredibly cold, even in summer. When I knew him living in northern England, I remember him wearing extra-long shirts to keep his rear-end warm in winter, and he was the one who taught me that the best way to wear a scarf is to criss-cross it across my chest.

Funnily, although I know he was in Canada during two summers, and I know how incredibly hot Canadian summers can be, for some reason I don't visualise him in summer, only in winter. Perhaps this is because he never spoke of summer with me – winter was the shocker for a country boy from Jamaica.

I envision him curling up most uncomfortably in a camp cot in the station dormitory, trying to fit his long, lanky frame into a bed made for mere mortals. Similarly, how on earth did he squeeze into the various cockpits, especially that of the Spitfire? This venture must truly have been a labour of determination, dedication, and discipline – he stuck with the Air Force for five years of his life.

> The following is an account by a New Zealander Ron Mayhill, who was stationed for a time in Brandon, Manitoba. He speaks of '…the friendly reception at Brandon. Brandon had military discipline, yet the instructors became friends. There are memories of ice-skating and being helped up by laughing girls, the staggering vastness of the prairies, the lakes a hundred miles north of Winnipeg, at Paulson, sixty degrees below freezing, frozen ear, the shock of double-glazed, heated rooms and venturing outside into the Arctic, the delight of many of our fellow New Zealanders and Aussies who had never seen snow before; and above all, the great comradeship which produced lifelong friendships' (Quoted in *Wings for Victory* by Spencer Dunmore, McLelland and Stewart, Inc., 1994, 228).

It was in Brandon, Manitoba during the summer of 1943 that Arthur Wint came into his own. Here, in Brandon, he learnt to fly, soaring above the clouds and experiencing freedom from Earth's gravity. Here, his commander James Baird commended him as a 'Very keen pilot who has worked hard all the way.' Another gruelling Canadian winter, and in summer of 1944 he made the hazardous Atlantic crossing to Britain, where he started advanced flight training. He earned the rank of Flying Officer, one of the first black officers in the RAF and he spent several months in advanced pilot training on various British bases, until in March of 1945 he began piloting Spitfires, the aircraft that epitomised the RAF in the

Second World War. When he eventually left the RAF in 1947, he held the rank of Flight Lieutenant.

He stood tall, elegant, distinguished in his RAF Flight Lieutenant's dress uniform. It was powder blue with the Wings on the left breast denoting a pilot. His cap sat at a jaunty angle, slanting down to the right. With his exceptionally long legs, he strode along the Strand in London, heading towards the West India Committee offices to collect his mail or to meet his brothers and other friends. He gazed over the heads of most people, while civilians as well as other service men and women regarded him with curiosity. They'd seen many service men and women of colour – they'd come from the Caribbean, from India, to help the Mother Country fend off the Germans, but they had never seen a black officer. They were not sure what to make of him. He, however, was not fazed by their curiosity. He walked through them secure in his personal power and strength.

Arthur may have finally found his calling as a leader of men, but the playful, skylarking attitude never really left him. As a trainee pilot in Canada, he once made a tricky, potentially lethal manoeuvre in his plane – an incident his brother Lloyd describes:

> Now I remember going somewhere and I was introduced to some Australians, and one of them he says 'Wint? Wint? You wouldn't happen to have a brother by the name of Arthur?' I say, 'Yes.' He says, 'The man is a madman!' I say, 'Why do you say that?' He says, 'He took off in a Tiger Moth [a training plane] and flew it straight up in the air.' But I say, 'The plane must stall on him.' He says, 'Yes, and he's taught that, but he flies the plane like

a madman.' So when I saw Arthur the next time I said, 'I met some Australians and they said that you're mad because you flew a Tiger Moth straight up. Why you do that?' He says, 'I just wanted to see what would happen.' Could have killed himself, you know. 'Cause if it stalls it starts to drop, tail raised, and it's hard to correct it. You ARE taught to stall it and start it up again, but under controlled conditions, but you know there's a limit to how much you can do it.

On another occasion, this time in Britain, Lloyd was stationed with the RAF in Weston Super Mare, on the Bristol Channel southwest of Bristol. The MP called him from the classroom to the gate, saying that an officer was there asking for him.

So I ask permission to leave and go to the gate and see your father standing up at the gate, no cap – it's a criminal sin for an officer to walk about camp without a cap. So I had to go and get out my spare cap and lend him – don't see it up to now! He had had a training flight in his Spitfire and he cooked the logbook – where he was supposed to go he didn't go, and he flew it to Bristol and took a taxi and came to my camp to look for me.

There is no mention of this incident in his logbook, so one assumes that his superior officers never found out.

A more serious occasion was on April 18, 1945 at Hawarden base in north Wales, when his comrades thought he had died. He had been flying a Spitfire and had landed in the slipstream of a Lancaster Bomber. The air sucking behind the big plane tipped him up so that he landed nose-down, damaging the nose and wing tip. His logbook states:

> At RAF Hawarden on 18th April 1945 failing
> to correct swing in time while landing a Spitfire
> aircraft, causing damage to the pilot and wing tip.
> Assessment: Carelessness. Punishment: Nil.

However, in order to get over the shock of that crash
and to ensure he did not lose his nerve, the ground crew
pulled him out of the plane, put him in another one and
sent him right back up. Unfortunately the others on the
base, particularly the Jamaicans, did not see him and
didn't know what had happened to him. They just saw the
crashed plane that he had been flying, so they assumed
that he was dead, and word spread rapidly through the
Jamaican community.

Lloyd:

> Your mother wrote me, sympathizing with me
> on the death of my brother. I was in Wales then
> and I said but I haven't heard this. So I went to
> the adjutant and I told him, I said my brother is a
> Spitfire pilot, stationed at Hawarden, and I've just
> got this letter from his girlfriend telling me that
> he has been killed. So I asked if he could check
> on it. A couple hours afterwards he called me and
> told me that he wasn't dead, he had a minor crash.
> Somebody even wrote to Mum in Jamaica about it.
> About a month afterwards she heard that it was a
> false rumour. But I ended up in a club that we used
> to go to quite regularly when we were in London
> and another fellow was there, Johnny Griffiths, and
> he was sitting beside me, a tall, dark fellow. And in
> walks your father, and this Johnny got up and said,
> 'See the man there who them say is dead!'

During the time they were all stationed in England during the War, Arthur and his brothers would try to get together whenever they could. However, Lloyd and Douglas were of lower rank than Arthur, who was a Flight Lieutenant. He was not supposed to fraternise with lower ranks – but of course, he did, literally, as they were his brothers. On one occasion the three were walking together on the Strand, en route to take a photograph to send home to their parents, when an RAF military police officer stopped Arthur to reprimand him. Lloyd goes on:

> And Arthur look around, and don't see anybody around, and tell him some class of bad wud, yu see! He says, 'These are my brothers, I'll have you know. I will walk anywhere with them regardless of what uniform they're wearing.'

Arthur demonstrated his family loyalty and disdain for commonly accepted mores on more than one occasion. Colour prejudice was something he could not abide. He was not as subject to it as others, because of his rank in the air force, and because of his celebrity as an athlete. So when his brother called on him to help deal with a case of racism he was experiencing, Arthur had no qualms about coming to his aid.

Lloyd, who was stationed in London at the time tells the tale:

> There was a little corporal and only three of us coloured people on the station – a Trinidadian Joe Hosein and myself, and an American fellow – the three of us came over together. This corporal decided to 'tek a set' on Joe Hosein and myself – you know, want to rag us and make us do extra

duties, just because we were different. And Arthur called to say that he was in London, so I say 'Do me a favour, come up here one afternoon.' And Arthur walked up and down in front of that corporal, and every time Arthur pass he have to jump and salute. I say 'You saluting a black man now!' And he stopped – [he was] different altogether when he saw Arthur with his wings, a Spitfire pilot, and the man never interfered with us again, so long as I was on that station.

Having been in the RAF was a major influence on my father's life. As with his athletics, I didn't really know many specifics about these years as I was growing up, but it is clear the RAF and the War were always invisible shadows lingering over our lives. I was born six years after hostilities ended and so never experienced the War first-hand. Certainly when our families got together however, it was obvious that those years and experiences – the War, the service, and subsequently post-war life in England – had a powerful effect not only on their worldview, but also their future professional lives.

The Wint brothers and Derry Marsh were not the only members of my family to serve in England during the War: my mother Norma was one of 24 young women who enlisted with the Auxiliary Territorial Services (ATS). My mother experienced great opposition from her parents, who could not understand her need to be involved in this, the 'greatest drama of our time,' but she was over 21 years old and did not need their permission, as did some of the other women. So in September 1943, a year after my father left Jamaica, the 24 women boarded the New Zealand merchant ship *Rimutaka* and set sail under convoy for England. Along with them were several New Zealand airmen and British soldiers returning from the Far East.

The ATS engaged women, mainly between the ages of 18 and 43, for non-combatant duties with military units during the War. The recruits included stenotypists, drivers – Princess Elizabeth was an ATS driver – and other services, and some of the women eventually became radar operators and mechanics. Many of the recruits – including my mother – worked in munitions plants getting weapons prepared for D-Day, June 6, 1944.

After four weeks at sea, *Rimutaka* docked under German bombing at Avonmouth in southwest England, not far from Weston Super Mare where Lloyd, and later Derry were stationed. Avonmouth experienced regular German attacks because of its strategic importance – it had extremely high and low tides, and the Luftwaffe were seeking to destroy the lock gates. My mother glosses over this landing under attack – she is more expressive about the bombings in London, when they had to take shelter in the Underground. It seems to me that she was so excited about arriving in England and the start of her new adventure, that the bombing was all part of this excitement.

After their initial military training in Guildford, at the end of which their squad won the marching competition, they were sent to Bicester – pronounced, in true British fashion 'Bister' – northeast of Oxford, where they worked at the depot responsible for motor transport and parts to be used on D-Day.

While in the ATS, the Jamaican women would go to London on leave, heading first of all to the West India Committee offices near the Strand to collect mail and news from home, and to connect with fellow Jamaicans serving in the Armed Forces.

In the eighteenth century, an association of London merchants who had business dealings with the West Indies formed the West India Committee. During the War, the Committee played a vital role for all personnel from the Caribbean area, offering their offices as an address at which personnel could receive mail. These offices were situated in central London on Norfolk Street, near the Strand, and it became the first place a service man or woman would head for on their day pass in London, to find out if there was any mail waiting for them. Unofficially these offices also became a great meeting place where personnel could exchange news – for instance news about those who had been killed or had gone missing. They could also read newspapers from home, while families from throughout Britain would write the West India Committee offering hospitality to Caribbean servicemen and women.

When the War in Europe ended on May 8, 1945, there were huge celebrations throughout Britain. The whole world seemed to go crazy with dancing, singing and parties in the street and celebration drinks. The dancing, singing and kissing and hugging of complete strangers carried on all evening. The cheering and flag waving was non-stop. My mother was part of that crowd, carried aloft on the euphoria outside Buckingham Palace where the King, Queen and the two Princesses came out onto the balcony. My father unfortunately was stationed in northern England at the time, and was not able to be in London to participate in the big celebration.

The Athlete

I've never seen my father run – at least not competitively. All his running fame came before I was born, or when I was still a small baby. I learnt that he was famous and an athlete by osmosis over the years, and knew that he had won two Olympic gold medals, but I never saw his prowess first-hand. Throughout my young life I never saw footage of his races, but I knew about them, especially the big ones.

So it was that sometime before the 1988 Olympics in Seoul my daughter Anna and I were watching an Olympic special on TV. It was a retrospective on the 1948 Games, and we knew from the description that they would be looking at that fateful relay in which he pulled up lame and lost the race.

As we got closer to the time, I became more and more tense. I was clutching a pillow to my chest and starting to hyperventilate. The race came on, and I started to sob uncontrollably. Anna was saying, 'Calm down, Mum,' but I couldn't calm down, because I knew what was going to happen and in part I didn't want to see it. This is a story I've heard throughout my life, but I had never actually seen it. Now it was real, made flesh. I saw my father fall on the field in agony, physical and emotional agony. He hopped off the track clutching the back of his leg, fell onto the inner field, and beat the grass with the baton. He and the other three runners – McKenley, Rhoden, Laing – were highly favoured to win this race, because my father and McKenley had already placed one and two in the 400 metres. The disappointment must have been overwhelming.

I've seen other runners fall, and because my father's story was always with me, I felt tremendous empathy for them – the New Zealand steeplechaser in the 1970 Commonwealth Games; Jamaican Bert Cameron in the 1984 Olympics; and Canadian hurdler Perdita Felicien who fell in the 2004 Athens Games. My father was devastated by the failed 4x400 metres attempt in 1948. He was a team player, who always wanted what was best for the team and was not simply seeking personal glory. He felt he had let down his team.

Only four days before the relay, Arthur had garnered silver in the 800 metres, coming in behind American rival Mal Whitfield, and thus winning Jamaica's very first ever Olympic medal. When asked to recall that race in a *Sports Illustrated* interview in 1983, my father explained the strategic mistake that prevented his winning the gold medal:

> It was a total error on my part. I should have won and broken the Olympic record. Marcel Hansenne of France had had the fastest time in the semis, so I decided I'd just shadow him. Whitfield ran around into the lead and I dismissed him. I didn't go after him. Then, when I saw he was getting away, I was boxed between two Frenchmen [Hansenne and Robert Chef d'hotel].

Two days later, on August 5, two days before the relay, my father and his teammate Herb McKenley ran in the final of the 400 metres. McKenley was highly favoured to win this race, and was very popular with Jamaicans at home. Throughout the War, he had been on a track scholarship in the US, and had been excelling in the 100, 200 and 400 metre races. Of course, being not so far from home, he had returned to Jamaica many times, and his successes in the US were well reported in Jamaica. Arthur had been away from Jamaica since 1942, and collective memory being short, not many people remembered his schoolboy athletic promise, or had heard about his triumphs on the amateur athletics circuit in Great Britain. He was now a relative unknown.

Arthur was running in second place behind Herb around the final curve, with Mal Whitfield (US) coming third. He was happy to come second to Herb. However, not too far from the finish line, Arthur realised that Herb was flagging, and he had a split-second decision to make. He had been content to let Herb win, but he was certainly not content to let Herb lose, to let Jamaica lose, nor to hand the race over to the American. So he sped up, passed McKenley, and so won Jamaica's first-ever Olympic Gold. McKenley says that he heard Arthur's thundering footsteps coming up behind him, closing the gap. He subsequently overtook his teammate and countryman to garner gold. The British spectators, along with the Jamaican and other Caribbean people in the stadium, all rose as one and cheered the one-two victory of Wint and McKenley. The photograph taken at the medal ceremony shows Arthur bending to have the medal placed around his neck. Herb is looking on from the number two spot, with a disappointed, almost bitter expression on his face. The gold had been snatched from him, but there was every hope for a gold in the relay.

Arthur had done what no other Jamaican had ever done before: he had won a gold medal at the Olympic Games. It was an exhilarating triumph. His teammate Herb McKenley had come in second, and together with George Rhoden and Les Laing, they intended to make new history this day, favoured, as they were to win the 4x400 metres relay. The only serious competition was the American team, and the Jamaicans had a fighting chance of beating them. Also because of the excitement of Arthur's earlier exploits in the Games and his fame in British amateur athletics, the British crowd was solidly behind them.

Early on the morning of Saturday, August 7, 1948, Arthur Wint got out of bed. It was a beautiful, warm morning, another in the string of hot, hazy days that Britain had been experiencing. It was a day that would remain with him for the rest of his life. It should have been a day of utter glory.

The Jamaican men took it easy that morning as they started their day in the former war barracks near Wembley Stadium. They went for a gentle walk to limber up, but no serious training that day. All the pre-race work would be mental. As they walked they talked about other matters not related to the race.

After a light lunch, they headed for the stadium to prepare, physically and mentally, for the challenge ahead. They dressed in their warm-up gear and went out to the area specifically designated for warm-ups. After about 45 minutes of jogging, they ran through their strategy for the race, and practised their baton changes. Back in the locker room, they showered and rubbed themselves down, changed into their cool, fresh race gear with 15 minutes to go before they had to report to the field. That quarter hour was spent in total relaxation. Arthur lay on the floor with his legs up the wall and his eyes closed, having arranged for someone to call him in time. He did not sleep during that time, but meditated. He would not have called it meditation in 1948, but in shutting out the exterior world, stilling his thoughts, and breathing deeply, he was in fact meditating. The other team members also relaxed in their own ways. This quiet time helped to focus their minds on the race.

The foursome headed out to the track to report for their race a little before 3:00 pm. There was quite a crowd waiting to run – as this was a race in which each person ran a quarter mile, one full lap of the track, all the runners were at or near the starting line. The Jamaicans offered best wishes to all their rivals, including the American team – a graciousness no longer seen in high performance sports today.

Roger Bannister, who later broke the four-minute mile record, knew Arthur well, and speaks of him in his autobiography *The Four-Minute Mile*. He calls the fated race 'perhaps the most moving and tragic moment of the whole Games.' He describes the race:

> Rhoden was the first runner for Jamaica and finished level with his American opponent, Harnden. The second Jamaican runner Laing, a sprinter gallantly trying to race twice his normal distance, handed over to Wint twelve yards behind Cochran, the American Olympic 400 metres hurdles champion.

Could Wint and McKenley win this margin back from Cochran and Whitfield? It seemed unlikely....
With enormous strides he flashed around the first bend. Normally Arthur Wint's running seemed deceptively slow, but this time there was no mistaking his speed and urgency.

As he entered the back straight he gained on Cochran with each stride, but suddenly his body convulsed and he flung himself on the grass verge, his face distorted with the agony of a searing muscle pull....I did not see Cochran steaming home to give Whitfield a commanding lead, but remained staring at the prostrate figure of Arthur Wint, thumping the turf with baton and fist in exasperation, oblivious to the comforting enquiries of his fellow Jamaicans.

Herb McKenley told me that when Arthur beat the track with the baton that was the closest to being angry he had ever seen him. McKenley had lost the 400 metres to him, which he had thought he was going to win:

I was extremely disappointed, to say the least. And then came the relay, and I wanted very much to show that my being beaten wasn't a matter of my not having [what it takes]. I was to get the baton from him, and then [he pulled up]. He hadn't gone very far, because he had just taken the baton. It happened around the middle of the turn. I think what happened is that the American had quite a bit of yardage on him. Arthur usually is a person who starts relatively slow, but he was running from day one this time, and I suppose he was probably not accustomed to get out so quickly. I think it might have been caused from his going out full blast immediately. That's probably what happened. And when I saw him, I was of a mind just to start running, then I said, 'what for? The man needs your support.' And I went over to him, and of course both of us started crying, and when the other two came all four of us were crying.

He had not only lost the race, he had let his team down. This, coupled with the pain in his leg, was more than he could bear. He crossed his arm across his eyes and leaned into Herb, sobbing on his shoulder. His brother Lloyd, who was in the stands watching the race, says he came down onto the field in concern for his brother:

When Arthur pulled his muscle in 1948 I was the first person on that track. I ran through the race. I ran down from my seat, the race was still going on, and I ran straight across the track. There are about three different newsreels of that, and there is one particular one, you'll see me in there in a brown suit. I picked him up off the ground. And nobody tried to stop me.

The medical team came out and carried Arthur off, accompanied by the other three very dejected relay athletes. Almost no one noticed the Americans winning the race.

Roger Bannister feels that Arthur had run too many races in too short a time, what with the various heats, semi-finals and finals, and was simply exhausted. McKenley feels he started out too fast when he received the baton from Laing, trying to close the gap with the American. His usual race strategy was to start relatively slowly, and to build up speed over the distance, but not this time. Whatever the reason, it was just too much, and his leg cramped.

That was the end of the 1948 Olympic Games for Arthur, but certainly not the end of his athletic career.

One might have thought that defeat and pain in what should have been the finest race of his life might have held my father back. Someone with less drive and self-determination would have called it quits. After all, he was in the throes of his medical studies, in themselves a major undertaking; London was still recovering from a crippling war and there were still hardships and rationing to deal with; and as of April 1949, he had a new wife at home. So who needed the aggravation of having to get to training when anatomy and a new wife were beckoning? However, he had let himself down. More importantly, he had let his team down, and for Arthur Wint that was simply not a situation he could leave unresolved. He had already in his 28 years experienced major tragedy and had risen from those ashes, so this defeat would not sideline him. Mike Fennel of the Jamaican Olympic Association says:

> Arthur Wint was always unquestionably acknowledged as a team man. He was not an individualistic person, he was always a team man, he was thinking of others and the team and so when as a part of the relay team he pulled up, Arthur's agony was not only for himself, but also for the team.

So he made his choice. Rather than quit he went back to his medical studies, and continued to train and compete around England, Europe, Africa, New Zealand, and elsewhere. He continued to run with his club, the Polytechnic Harriers, and with the University of London team until 1953. He and my mother finally got together and married in 1949, and eventually I came along in late 1951.

Apart from a couple of meets in Canada while he was training as a pilot, my father did not compete in any major events between 1942 and 1944. However, shortly after arriving in Britain with the RAF, my father met fellow half-miler Doug Wilson, who introduced Arthur to the Polytechnic Harriers athletics club, a club he would be associated with for the next several years. He took part in many meets, including one in 1946 as part of an Amateur Athletics Association (AAA) team against Cambridge University, in which he won the 440 and 880 yards titles, and cleared six feet (1.83 metres) in his first try at high jump in months. He went on to run in meets representing the Polytechnic Harriers, the AAA, the RAF, and London University, as well as at various charitable events in Britain and Europe. He was rapidly becoming a darling of British athletics, ranking along with Roger Bannister – who would later break the four-minute mile – and Trinidadian sprinter and fellow RAF 'Poly' member McDonald Bailey, as a member of what Mel Watman (quoted in *Black Sportsmen* by Ernest Cashmore, Routledge, 1982) called the 'Holy Trinity' of athletics, a reign that would be crowned in Gold only two years later at the London Olympics.

My father was a beautiful though unusual runner, typically running with both his shoulders and thumbs up. Many have commented on not only his height of 6 feet 5½ inches, but on his extraordinarily long stride – about nine feet in length. Roger Bannister, his friend and rival in the 880 yards, found my father's stride very off-putting – his stride was too long to match step for step, but not long enough to take two steps to each of his one, so that it would throw Bannister – and other shorter runners – out of rhythm.

One writer, David Thurlow in *Track Stats* describes my father's style:

> When he began to run it was his stride – around 9ft and a bit – and his arm action which suggested in moments of extreme fatigue or stress as he neared the tape that he was trying to knock himself out.

> So magnificent was his stride that it sometimes made spectators gasp and laugh in amazement. And there was the deceptive power. He never seemed to be putting great effort into his running, but that was an illusion. He was covering the ground at an incredible speed, fast enough to win Jamaica's first Olympic individual gold medal: 400 metres in 46.2 in 1948.

He was also a strategic runner, visualising and plotting his plan of action well before an event. My mother recalls that he drew a track on the wall of their bathroom and marked each place where he would change tactics. This habit of visualising a future event is a method that he would carry over to his medical and surgical careers, going over how to treat a case or mentally doing the surgery step by step. It is also a strategy that today is being taught to athletes both elite and amateur.

However, he was notorious for not 'overtraining.' He apparently used to say of himself that he was a 'lazy athlete.' Doug Wilson says, in an interview with another of my father's friends and rival half-miler, John Parlett, that

...he certainly wasn't known for his training, no. I think he put it at a minimum, I think he just got by with it. He just had a terrific amount of natural ability. But I don't think he was one of the world's great trainers, no. He was however, a very good club man indeed. Although later on he would engage in the international matches, he always turned out for the club. He captained the club on various occasions, particularly on our tour of Sweden.

Wilson wasn't the only one to notice my father's lack of training – several of his peers have commented on it, and the *Gleaner's* London correspondent mentioned in June 1949:

There was some doubt whether the Jamaican's training was sufficiently advanced to deal with the American challenger [D. Bolen] in an international match at White City Stadium. After one false start, the runners were off, and Wint's long streaking stride was again seen in action. Turning into the straight, he led Bolen by three yards, but the American was creeping up again as they neared the tape.

The Jamaican's incomplete training was telling, but his muscle symphony action, as perfect as ever, carried him on to the tape to win by one yard.

As much as he might have depended on natural ability, my father was always concerned about the condition of his legs – he was plagued throughout his athletic career by hamstring issues. Consequently, according to John Parlett, my father devised a special contraption to help with his physical conditioning, a device his clubmates called 'Arthur's Board.' This was a plank with a broom handle across the back. He would lie back on it and he could alter the angle at which he then had to raise his legs from the board over the back of his head. 'The idea,' says Parlett, 'was to strengthen the stomach muscles and the leg muscles, because Arthur Wint had these great long legs and he needed to strengthen them.' Compared with training strategies of nowadays, training in the 1940s and 1950s was relatively primitive. As another of my father's peers puts it, 'The main way one trained was by running and very little by way of bodybuilding, which was then in its infancy.'

Another way my father dealt with his problem of pulled muscles was to try to run on the outside of the track, rather on the inside. Tony Watts, who had been a colleague at the University of London Athletics Club says in his interview with John Parlett:

> But the great thing about Arthur was that he was always worried about pulling muscles, which people remember did occur in the Olympic Games relay, and he said that one of the problems about running on the inside lane in a quarter mile race as it was, or the 400 metres, was that his legs had a greater strain, so he liked to run as far out as possible. Another aspect of his running on the inside lane was that he also had this problem, with such long legs, that sometimes he stepped on the curb on the inside and this caused him to fall once or twice.

Yet my father truly enjoyed running, that is certain, as he always travelled with his spikes and would seek out the local running club. Perhaps more than running, he enjoyed the camaraderie of the team. When Herb McKenley commented that his time for the half-mile would have been even better if he had trained in the US, my father replied, 'But I would have had half the fun.' Fun was definitely part of his repertoire – travelling to interesting places, singing with his teammates as they waited for a bus or train, drinking a beer after a track meet, spontaneous get-togethers at my parents' flat – these were part and parcel of his running culture.

With his physical stature and unusual running style, and with his domination at the track, Arthur Wint rapidly became a media darling. In Britain of the late 1940s and early 1950s, in the absence of widespread television, track meets were a popular pastime, and along with sprinter McDonald Bailey, Arthur joined the ranks of the British track stars. Doug Wilson comments, 'He and McDonald Bailey...they were always around together. I would say that between them – together and individually – they must have attracted thousands and thousands to the White City during that period.' There is a touching photograph of my father from that era, in which he is surrounded by eager little boys clamouring for an autograph, such was his popularity.

Over the years that he ran in Great Britain and internationally, my father won a great many trophies. One such was apparently an odd-looking pottery parrot that he won on a European trip. John Parlett tells how my father deliberately left this prize behind in his hotel room with the hope that it would disappear, but one of the hotel staff discovered it and rushed up to bring it to Arthur before he left. I have no idea where that parrot is now, because I have never seen it.

My mother has kept many of my father's trophies, as well as medals and other beautiful mementos from these travels, but two trophies lived with us on a daily basis for many years. One trophy was a doll from Czechoslovakia (as it then was) that sat on top of our piano. She stood about 18 inches tall, and was dressed in traditional Czech dress – headscarf, white long-sleeved blouse, and a dress and long vest of handwoven material in reds and greens. She lived for a long time, first on my grandparents' piano and then on ours when we returned to Jamaica in 1963, but she unfortunately succumbed to damage from insects. The other trophy that still sits in my mother's living room is the mahogany bust my father was given when he ran in Nigeria. My sisters and I lovingly call her Matilda – or 'Miss Mattie.' She is a woman with strong African features – high cheekbones, beautiful lips, but it is her hair that amazes. For years we couldn't figure out how her hair was styled, until cane rows came into fashion in the late 1970s, and then we had an 'Ah ha' moment: Matilda has four or five thick cane rows that culminate in a little flip of plaits at the nape of her neck. She is stunning.

The 1952 Olympics eventually came along, held in Helsinki, Finland, and as team captain my father proudly carried the Jamaican flag during the opening ceremony. In 1952, according to Mike Fennel, there was more anxiety about Herb McKenley, because he had not yet won a gold medal: he kept falling short. He ran the 100 metres and there was a very close finish with the American Remigino – in the video Remigino is actually seen congratulating

McKenley. However, the result was disputed, because it was a photo finish and Lindy Remigino was ultimately awarded the gold. A lot of Jamaicans, according to Mike Fennell,

> felt that Herb should have had the nod, or at worst, it should have been a dead heat, but they gave the race to Remigino, and that dictated the whole perception of what was going on – that Herb was 'denied' a gold medal, so a lot of attention was being paid to that.

In 1952 Arthur was less than stellar in the 400 metres, placing fifth and seeing first and second go to George Rhoden and Herb McKenley. In the 800 metres, Arthur again came second to American Mal Whitfield. The focus was now on the relay – could the team redeem themselves after the 1948 debacle? Could Herb McKenley finally win a gold medal?

In the 4x400 metres relay the running order was changed from that of 1948: this time Arthur started, giving him the opportunity to use his traditional strategy of starting relatively slowly and building speed over the 400 metres. He handed over to Laing and when McKenley took the baton for the third lap, he was several metres behind the leading American. He put on an exceptional spurt, running 'like a man inspired' (to quote the newsreel commentator). When he handed the baton to Rhoden for the final leg, McKenley was fractionally ahead. Rhoden pulled out in front and stayed there for the entire lap, to ultimately beat the Americans and win the race. In finally earning his long-awaited gold medal, McKenley had run the fastest 400 metres, in a time of 44.6 seconds – a time that would have been a world record for an individual 400-metre race, a record that would have stood until 1976 (not including Lee Evans's 1968 record at altitude in Mexico.) Overall, the 'Helsinki Quartet' as they became known, set a new record of 3:03.9, smashing the previous record by 4.3 seconds.

The stadium in Helsinki erupted when Rhoden crossed the finish line. Afterwards in their dressing room, the quartet celebrated their incredible comeback victory by drinking rum from toothbrush tumblers – joined in this toast by a proud young Prince Phillip, Duke of Edinburgh. Not only had Herb McKenley earned his gold medal in spectacular fashion, but Arthur Wint had also vindicated himself and his athletic reputation.

My father continued to run in various meets in Great Britain and elsewhere, but his medical studies were coming to an end, he was by now 32 years old, and starting to consider his next move – returning to Jamaica to practise medicine. Thus in 1952 he made the choice to run his last races at the White City stadium – a 440-yards and a medley relay. Following these events, he ran a lap of honour during which he received a standing ovation from the appreciative and very loyal fans.

The Helsinki Quartet was the talk of Kingston and all of Jamaica. They were to be honoured again years later when Jamaica gained independence and the National Stadium was built, in 1962. At that time all four athletes were brought back to Kingston to be a major part of the dedication and opening of the Stadium, and the unveiling of the statue that proudly guards the entrance. *The Athlete* was sculpted by Alvin Marriott based on an award-winning photograph of my father leaping forward from the starting blocks. It is said to be a combination of my father's body and McKenley's head, but I see all Arthur in this striking, iconic work – the long, sinewy muscles in his arms and legs, the thrust back of the upper arm, the thrust forward of the lower arm, the hands held loosely, no tension, the back foot pushing off the block while the front foot has just been lifted for the first stride, the head raised to look towards the goal, purposeful, sure, strong. This statue has always filled me with pride, and is a fitting tribute to my father, his colleagues, and all the outstanding Jamaican athletes who have followed in their footsteps.

Wedding, Honeymoon and Early Marriage

The relationship between Norma and Arthur continued on and off through the War years. They corresponded while he was in Canada, giving each other information about their lives but not really being romantic. They met again when my father was posted to England in 1944. He had completed his initial training in Canada, had received his commission, and was now stationed at a base in Surrey, while my mother was stationed with the ATS at Bicester, near Oxford.

Shortly after arriving in Britain, Arthur travelled up to Bicester to see Norma. No doubt she had been very strong in his mind and heart during the long, bitterly cold winters and hot summers of Saskatchewan and Manitoba. He must have worried about her safety when he heard she would be going to England, with its air raids and rationing. For her part, she was very happy to see him, this 'long-foot bwoy' with whom she had formed a bond back home, and found him very smart and dashing in his RAF officer's uniform, hat set at a rakish angle. However, she was not ready for the next step in the relationship:

> He wanted us to get engaged, but I was not so sure at this time, even though there were deep feelings on both sides. We talked a lot, but no commitment

was made. During the next few years we'd meet intermittently with our mutual friends, but the subject was not brought up again.

Norma wasn't ready to settle down yet. The mind-opening and heightened awareness of living in a country at war made her realise that she wasn't ready to make a permanent commitment at that time. Arthur had been her first boyfriend. He had been her only boyfriend – other boys had kept their distance because he was involved with her. Now she felt restricted, and wanted some freedom to experience life. She wasn't seeing anyone else, 'I had lots of boyfriends but no one special,' and she wanted to be able to travel with her girlfriends. In fact, during the War, they would travel to Cornwall, Scotland and to neutral Ireland, and after the War was over, in summer of 1947 a group went to Prague for the first Festival of the World Federation of Democratic Youth. The festival was held there in remembrance of the events of October and November 1939, when thousands of young Czechs rose in demonstrations against the occupation of the country by Nazi Germany. The motto of the festival was 'Youth Unite, Forward for Lasting Peace!'

Norma's rejection of Arthur at this point would, I imagine, have been quite devastating. He had left Jamaica two years before and had kept her in his heart all this time. He was doing well in the Air Force and felt it was time now to settle down. He was 24 years old and the War didn't look as though it would end any time soon, so he wanted to move ahead with creating a family. Despite that, he agreed with Norma that they should take a break from each other. They did, however, stay in touch, and would meet up in

London from time to time when they went to the West India Committee to pick up their mail. They would also meet at private parties, and they maintained a friendship but nothing more. It would be four more years before they really reconnected. He left the RAF in 1947 and started his medical studies, continuing his athletics, while she went to college studying to be a Chartered Company Secretary. During the 1948 Olympics in London, where Arthur won his first gold medal, Norma was an attaché to the Jamaican Women's Team, and so was part of the excitement of that great event.

After having rejected Arthur's proposal back in 1944, Norma had lain to rest the travel bug that had infected her, and by 1948 she was now ready to settle down. Late in the year, close to Christmas, the West Indian men who lived at Knutsford House in London held a dance party that both Norma and Arthur attended. After the party, as Arthur was walking Norma back to her flat in Gloucester Place, she told him she'd had a change of heart and wanted to accept his proposal. He said nothing until they arrived at her flat, when he told her that he still cared for her, but only as he would care for a sister. 'I had my comeuppance,' says my mother, 'and I was very upset.' Her brother Chappie was by that time also living at Gloucester Place, and so she spoke to him, told him how devastated she was. 'I think Chappie must have spoken to him,' she says. 'I think he told Arthur he was being silly talking about caring for me as a sister, when he knew he had deeper feelings than that.'

However, by her twenty-eighth birthday in January 1949, nothing concrete had happened between them. So, having finished her course, and with no marriage proposal in sight, she decided to return to Jamaica. Her friends held a birthday-cum-farewell party in her honour, to which Arthur was, of course, invited.

Arthur had been with Michael Manley and his then wife Jacqueline for dinner that evening, and so came late to the party with Carmen Manley, Douglas Manley's wife. When she arrived, Carmen hinted to Norma that she thought something might be brewing with Arthur. He called Norma out onto the landing and asked her then and there to marry him. It seems Michael Manley had convinced him he was letting a good opportunity pass him by, and that he'd better do something about it or Norma would return to Jamaica and he would lose her forever. So the farewell party turned into a joyous engagement party.

They set a date to be married on April 6 that same year. The arrangements were very hurried, as this was the only time Arthur could get away from both studies and athletics.

My mother's great lifelong friend, Ivy Murray Thompson lived in England. Her husband Wade was also in the RAF, and they had two daughters at the time, Madge and Ann. When my parents decided to get married, 'Ivy was head cook and bottle-washer,' says Norma. It was Ivy who sewed my mother's dress, and when the cakes arrived from Jamaica, baked by Grandma McBean and S'Ene, it was Ivy who iced them. She was also the Matron of Honour while her daughters were the flower girls. My mother wore lilies of the valley in her hair, and carried a bouquet of white lilies. My father wore his RAF dress uniform. Together they made a stunningly beautiful couple.

Chappie 'gave away' my mother, standing in for her beloved BC. In the car on the way to the church, Norma was nervous and excited, worried that she was going to be late. She kept telling the driver to hurry, but Chappie quietly told him 'go slowly, go slowly.' Norma's good friend Faye Lindo selected the music, and my mother entered the church to the strains of Bach's 'Jesu Joy of Man's Desiring.' There is a photograph, perhaps my favourite, which shows my parents in the car just after the ceremony, waving to their friends. Their smiles are wistful and just a little tentative, maybe concerned about what their life together might bring.

After the service, a reception was held at Gloucester Place. The landlady gave over the drawing room with its parquet floor for the reception itself, while Norma's great friend Phyllis MacPherson – who would later be one of my godmothers – organised a group of women to make sandwiches and drinks. Don Mills – later my godfather – gave the toast to the couple.

While my parents got married in England, their friends and relatives in Jamaica had a party in their honour at the Marsh home.

After the wedding they honeymooned in Paignton, Devon, where my father had previously run in athletics meets. They had friends there, who took them to the various historic sites, and the Paignton Athletics Club gave them a wedding present of a crystal water jug with glasses that my mother still has.

During the first night of their honeymoon, my parents scarcely had time to sleep (or anything else) because they were waiting for a long-distance call from my mother's parents BC and S'Ene in Jamaica. Every couple of hours they were called down to the hotel lobby to receive this call, which did not actually come through until the next afternoon. Nowadays we don't really understand what a production it was to make or receive long-distance phone calls: they were not only difficult to make, but reception was often bad and they were very expensive. Consequently, people of my mother's era tended to be thrown off-balance by long-distance calls – their first thought was that there was something amiss.

Once they had received the call they were finally able to relax and enjoy their all-too-short hiatus from the real world, exploring Devon and revelling in each other. It would be a long while before they had another such break, as married life galloped on, taking strides into the future, long strides like my father's.

After the euphoria of the wedding and honeymoon, it was back to 'real' life, living together in the boarding house near Finsbury Park in the northern part of London where Arthur had lived alone. My father was studying medicine and training, while my mother had started to work as a Company Secretary with an employment agency, working in various firms around London, and eventually settling with the BBC. They started looking for a flat of their own, only to get the kind of the racist runaround one witnessed in the film *To Sir With Love* – 'Sorry, it's already been taken.' Eventually they found a flat in Philbeach Gardens near the Earls Court Tube Station, a nexus of lines on the underground railway, and very convenient. They were living in just one room then at Finsbury Park, and the flat seemed to be beyond their means. My mother was working and my father was on scholarship, and when they looked at the finances they felt it would cost too much.

My mother tells me

> So I went to bed and next morning when I woke up, Arthur had gone to college, but he had left a note on my pillow, showing me how if we did this, and we did that, we could just do it. And we did. He figured it out that this was the flat for us, because what we liked about it mainly was that we were completely on our own. We moved in there in '49 I think, the same year we were married and we kept that flat until '63, when we came back to England.

This flat stayed in the family for years – they eventually bought it. It was to this flat that I came as a baby from hospital, and I actually have a couple of memories of living there – sitting in a high-chair as my mother read to me; walking on a harness and getting away from her to run through the snow (my birthday is in November, so I must have been just over two when this happened). Various family members and friends used the flat over the years, and when we returned to England when I was seven, we lived there for a short while before moving to Altrincham in the north.

During the years at Philbeach Gardens, my father continued to study and to run in various meets, at White City Stadium, Motspur Park and elsewhere, and my mother often went to see him run. They made friends with other athletes – John Parlett, a fellow half-miler who won gold in the 1950 Commonwealth Games, and who remains a friend to this day; Roger Bannister, who shattered the four-minute-mile record; Harold Moody, a shotputter; and Harold Abrahams of *Chariots of Fire* fame, among many others. In addition, many of their Jamaican friends were in England studying, including my mother's brothers, Chappie and Derry, as well as other great lifelong friends. Along with the Jamaicans and other West Indians, there were also students from Africa. The world was beginning to take on a new shape as former colonies struggled towards independence. Many of my parents' friends and acquaintances went on to become political and academic leaders in their various countries, heading the move to independence from British rule that took hold in the 1950s. Arthur and Norma were part of this 'Brave New World' full of possibilities.

Having come to Britain during the War, my parents were in the vanguard of black settlement there. Major migration from Jamaica and other British Caribbean territories to Great Britain, started with the *MV Windrush*, which brought 492 Jamaicans to Britain in July 1948. The idea was to boost the workforce in the post-war rebuilding process, and Britain tapped into the unemployment and lack of adequate opportunities in the Caribbean:

> If it hadn't been for the Second World War, the *Windrush* and her passengers might not have made the voyage at all. During the war, thousands of Caribbean men and women had been recruited to serve in the armed forces.
>
> When the *Windrush* stopped in Jamaica to pick up servicemen who were on leave from their units, many of their former comrades decided to make the trip in order to rejoin the RAF. More

> adventurous spirits, mostly young men, who had
> heard about the voyage and simply fancied coming
> to see England, 'the mother country,' doubled their
> numbers. (From *'Windrush* – A Celebration' by
> Mike Phillips. Written to accompany the BBC
> *Windrush* season, Summer 1998.)

I have seen video of the arrival of these new immigrants to Britain, mostly men but a few women and some families, wide-eyed with wonder and excitement at the beginning of their new adventure.

Most of these new arrivals went to work in the public service – in the post office, hospitals, London Transport and the railways. There was plenty of work but they found it difficult getting accommodation, so they were put up in a deep air raid shelter close to the labour exchange in Brixton, and as a result, this neighbourhood became their home. It is still home today to the descendents of the original immigrants, as well as newer immigrants.

My parents were not close to these newcomers, as they moved in entirely different circles. They would, however, encounter them as bus drivers, postal workers and in other vocations as they moved around London. Some of the anti-black prejudice that resulted from this influx of 'foreigners' would have found its way into my parents' lives. Yet these 'coloured' people from the colonies were now part of the British landscape, bringing a not-always-welcome diversity to British life, and this diversity would only grow over the coming years as others migrated to Britain.

The *Windrush* passengers would have closely followed the exploits of the tall athlete from home who was making such an impact. In fact they had arrived only days before the start of the 1948 Olympics, so they could not escape being drawn into the excitement of my father's gold medal – and the disappointment of my father's failure in the relay.

From late December 1950 to early January 1951, my father travelled to Christchurch, New Zealand to participate in the Centennial Games. En route there and back the team made stops in Australia and the US, where they participated in various meets. My father once again beat his friend and rival American Mal Whitfield in New Zealand. Later in 1951, my father and McDonald Bailey were invited to Nigeria and Ghana, receiving VIP treatment. It was during this trip that my father received 'Miss Matilda' the mahogany bust that sits in my mother's living room. My father was also given a horsehair whip, which I understand is the symbol of a chief of a particular nation in Nigeria – so he was therefore made an honorary chief. This in itself was a great honour, but it is an ironic one, as family legend has it that the original African from whom the Wints are descended, was from Nigeria. It is said he was never a slave, and our interpretation of that is that either he arrived in Jamaica after slavery was abolished, or that he was a chief in his country, and therefore was never formally enslaved. I don't know how realistic this is, but it is a beautiful story, one that may explain my father's natural sense of self-esteem and dignity.

Arthur and Norma maintained very close ties to Jamaica, and so when the Category Four Hurricane Charlie hit the island in August 1951, naturally they felt very distant and isolated. They were helpless as they heard of the devastation and the more than 150 deaths and thousands left homeless. They had no way to know how their own friends and families had fared.

In 2004, the *Daily Gleaner* ran an article entitled 'Hurricane Charlie Revisited – August 17, 1951' looking at the dreadful event:

> At 8:30 that night [August 17] Hurricane Charlie struck, unleashing its fury with 125-mile per hour winds and rain. In its aftermath, the hurricane left 154 people dead, 25,000 victims homeless and a decimated Banana and Coconut industry with the downing of trees in three parishes while, water, telephone and telegraph services were disrupted and roads made impassable.

> The hurricane levelled houses, wrecked ships at port, destroyed the Palisadoes Airport instalment and the Victoria pier. A collapsed dormitory at the General Penitentiary allowed 76 convicts to escape. They, along with other unlawful entities, would later wreak havoc on Kingston's business district with rampant looting.

> The hardest hit parishes were St Thomas, Kingston, St Andrew, St Catherine and Clarendon with Port Royal being completely destroyed for the third time in its history. The Corporate Area [Kingston and St Andrew] had over 12,000 people homeless, StThomas 10,000 and 3,000 elsewhere in the island. In total, over £16 million worth of damage was done and it took the island over five years to fully recover from the effects.

A few years ago in Toronto I met a man who is of Indian background and speaks with an English accent. In appearance he reminded me strongly of my uncles Lloyd and Douglas. I asked him when he had lived in England, and he said he was there during the early 1950s. So I said, 'A man of colour living in London in the 1950s – you would probably know of my father.' He stopped what he was doing and turned to face me. 'Wait a minute. Wint. You're Arthur Wint's daughter?'

'Yes,' I replied.

'I saw him run at White City,' he said. 'I saw him run the year of the hurricane in Jamaica. After the meet, your father went into the spectators with a hat, and collected money to send to Jamaica for the hurricane. I remember him well!'

My Uncle Lloyd was also in the stands that day at White City, and was one of those passing the hat:

> Arthur spoke, and he said he was trying to get some contributions to send to Jamaica because of this damaging hurricane that had demolished the place. And he asked other Jamaicans in the audience if they would assist in collecting the money. I was the one with the hat. I didn't know where to put the money, because the hat was so full, overflowing.

Later that year in November, I was born at St Bartholomew's Hospital where my father was studying. My mother tells the story:

> It was an exciting time looking forward to our baby's birth, so much so that when I was ready to go into hospital we completely forgot about phoning for an ambulance (even though the number was fixed by the phone) and went by taxi. But all went well and Valerie Elaine arrived....I had to get used to pushing the pram, and I suddenly developed

friends everywhere. Before Valerie's arrival we hardly knew our neighbours, now everyone would stop to say something. Babies and dogs are passports in England. We welcomed the change.

The excitement of a new marriage and a new baby did not stop my father's trajectory. He somehow managed to continue his medical studies – even winning a prize for surgery from St Bartholomew's – and to keep up with his athletic training. His goal was to run in the 1952 Olympics in Helsinki, determined to erase the memory of the 4x400 metre relay disaster of 1948. The young couple eked out an existence on his scholarship. My mother was no longer working now that she had a baby, and so the very timely financial donations from her Uncle George in the US also came in handy.

Their life together was hectic, to say the least. Between his studies and athletic training, and my mother's job and later a new baby, they had very little spare time. In 1952 he redeemed his athletic reputation by helping his team win the 4x400 metres relay in Helsinki, as well as garnering silver in the 800 metres. He graduated in 1953 as a medical doctor, and went on to do his internship at St Bartholomew's. My father's athletic prowess and popularity had made him a celebrity in the British sports world, his exploits carried in the media – the national newspapers and cinema newsreels – and eventually Buckingham Palace became aware of him. In 1954 he was honoured with an MBE, Member of the British Empire in the Queen's Honours List, for these athletic achievements and for his public service to Jamaica, and so my parents were invited to tea at Buckingham Palace.

My mother describes it:

> For such a special event we immediately started
> planning to do it in true Jamaican 'braggadocio'
> style (full of oneself). I would get a swanky outfit,
> while Arthur would get fitted out with proper attire,
> hired from Moss Bros., the well-known firm for
> such events. We would hire a car. However when
> we added it all up, 'braggadocio' went through
> the window. It would be lounge suit for him and
> I would wear a dress I had recently got from the
> States. The feeling nevertheless was that this was
> not the done thing. After arriving in our taxi, we
> saw couples hopping off buses in their finery, or
> coming up from the underground station. We got a
> lesson in values that afternoon!

It was a very colourful scene on the Palace grounds,
with people from various countries in national dress, and
English folk looking their very best. The gardens were
beautiful. Courtiers preceded the royal party, quickly
deciding who would be presented and positioning them in
certain spots to meet the royals.

My parents were among those selected to meet the
royal party, because my father had made such an impression
on the British public as an athlete and gentleman, and was
very popular at the time. Of course, he had already shared a
drink with Prince Phillip, in the dressing room in Helsinki!

It was not long after their presentation at Buckingham
Palace that my parents finally returned to Jamaica – with
me along of course – and my father moved into the next
phase of his career.

Return to Jamaica 1954

I was about three and we were still living in London when we got the news that my grandmother S'Ene had cancer and was not expected to live much longer. My mother and I flew to Jamaica when we heard. I remember being in the plane, and then arriving at a hospital with a wide entry staircase and pillars alongside the steps. Many years later as an adult, I visited a friend in hospital and recognised it – my mother confirmed that it was Nuttal Hospital in Cross Roads, Kingston. S'Ene was in bed and very happy to see us. She had had a dress made for me that I still remember: white piqué cotton with a pocket in the skirt, and with a man and woman appliquéd on the pocket. I regret that I never got to know her – she died shortly after we saw her that day. I'm told I look like her.

My mother and I stayed on in Jamaica after S'Ene's death, joined a short while later by my father. We went to live in a big house on Beechwood Avenue in Kingston – my mother, my father and me, along with our extended family: Uncle Chappie and his new English wife Jean; Blossom, a teenaged cousin; at one point my Uncle Derry and Aunt Monica; and of course my great-grandmother Grandma McBean. This was the woman I also came to call Grandma, and she remained a major part of our lives until she died when I was thirteen. By the time my sister Alison came along in 1956, Grandma's vision was beginning to fail – Alison was the last of her great-grandchildren that she was able to see. I gather from my mother that she had been a very active woman, but I knew her as very quiet and sedentary – her blindness completely sidelined her and robbed her of all the activities that she had enjoyed. I recall her sitting in a rocking chair, or sitting on the side of her bed combing her hair – it reached all the way down her back, and she would plait it and wrap the plait round and round into a bun at the back of her head, held in place with pins and combs.

My father went to work at the recently-opened University of the West Indies Hospital, also lecturing in anatomy in the Faculty of Medicine. Meanwhile my mother worked in the office of the Registrar at the University. The University is on the same site as the Gibraltar Camp that held refugees during the War, and many of the buildings dated from the Camp days. This is when I start to be conscious of my life, at about age four – I started school, had a best friend, and a big family all around, the only child at the time.

The house was always full of friends and family, as it was a great hub of social activity. I have strong memories of the vibrant and sometimes very loud veranda debates at Beechwood Avenue. I have no details at all, I was too young to understand, but the adults would always discuss the stories of the day after dinner and on Sundays, a drink of rum and ginger in hand. No doubt they argued about the latest on Jamaica's bid to form a Caribbean Federation; or what was happening with Norman Manley or Alexander

Bustamante; or the huge train crash at Kendal; or the polio outbreak.

My birthday parties were grand affairs on the front lawn. My parents had many friends and acquaintances, as well as other family members, who also had children about my age, so all these children would be invited. We would carry chairs out to the lawn, and set up a table with a lovely cake, and my mother would organise games such as musical chairs.

We kept chickens at the back of the Beechwood Avenue house, and on Sundays, Winston our gardener would kill one for lunch, which my father, the surgeon-in-training, would carve. We would regularly churn our own ice cream in a bucket – I got to turn the handle sometimes. We made all the exotic flavours that have become the norm today – coconut, rum and raisin, guava, mango, soursop.

In addition to Winston, we had a domestic helper, Miss Lyneth, who lived in a little house attached to the garage. She eventually married Ozzie who moved in with her there. Ozzie was a migrant worker who went to Florida regularly for months at a time to work in sugar and citrus. We also had a nanny who helped look after my sisters and me when they came along. Miss Lyneth stayed with the family for many years, until she migrated to the US and Ozzie's niece Nova took over. Nova is still looking after my Uncle Chappie today. It was the norm back then for middle class Jamaicans to have a number of servants, but looking back from the vantage point of today, it does seem a bit extravagant.

Due to his job, my father was often away from home. I have more memories of Jean and Chappie during these years than of my father, but there are a few poignant memories of Daddy that stick.

I once got hold of a curtain-ring and put it on my ring finger, parading around and showing off my 'wedding ring' to everyone in the house. Of course it got stuck, and just would not come off no matter what I did. My father tried soap, he tried oil, but to no avail – my finger just kept swelling. Uncle Chappie tried using a hacksaw, but I screamed and carried on so much that he had to abort that effort. Eventually my father took me up to University Hospital where a surgeon friend of his put me under ether and sawed the ring off my finger. I remember waking at one point when the ether mask must have slipped from my face, and feeling happy and reassured to see my father standing by the door, a tall figure in a white gown and mask.

When I was about five or six years old, the Coney Island Circus came to Kingston. This was such a unique and exciting event that of course we had to go. I was enthralled – particularly with the beautiful girl on the tightrope. I loved her appearance, her sparkly tutu, and the grace with which she walked carefully, balancing with her long pole, along the high tightrope. The next day I was telling my neighbour about this lovely vision, and decided to demonstrate. I took my shoes off and started to walk along the top of the barbed-wire fence. In my socks. Needless to say, I fell, and in doing so ripped my left leg badly. My father cleaned the wound and bandaged it with great care – and then gave me a good talking-to about how silly I had been. The most humiliating part of this episode was having to go to ballet class – which I hated already – in my short ballet dress with the bandaged leg in clear view. I still bear the scar.

While we were living at Beechwood Avenue, my mother had two more babies – Alison Jean in 1956, and Colleen Marie in 1958.

When my mother went to hospital to have my sister Alison – who nearly arrived at a 1956 Boxing Day party – my father took me to visit his parents in Cascade, Hanover, in the northwest of the Island. Granddad Wint, or 'Parson' as many called him, was the Presbyterian Minister in Cascade. This place was as different from our home in Kingston as could be imagined, for a five-year-old. The Manse was a big old house, with no electricity at the time, so lamps were needed at night – very exotic to me, the little urban girl. There were many more mules and donkeys than in the city, almost no motor cars, and the women carried their heavy loads to market on their heads. We walked to my grandfather's church across a large field on Sunday morning. We stayed in Cascade for several days, and the main thing I can remember from that time is my father valiantly trying to comb my unruly hair. This was one of the few times when I had my Daddy all to myself.

In 1957 there was an outbreak of Poliomyelitis in Jamaica, an acute viral disease that is one of the most dreaded childhood diseases. It paralyses those affected, usually in one leg. The Salk anti-polio vaccine had become available a few years earlier, and so with this outbreak, my father brought the vaccine home and vaccinated us all. When it came his turn, it was Uncle Chappie who injected him.

Arthur in his RAF uniform

The iconic photograph of Arthur, on which the statue at the National Stadium is based

The Jamaican Olympic 4x400m relay team: Les Laing, George Rhoden, Arthur Wint, and Herb McKenley

Arthur and Herb McKenley share a moment

*Arthur carrying the Jamaican flag at the 1952
Olympic Games in Helsinki*

Arthur, accompanied by the 'Helsinki Quartet', has the honour of lighting the Azteca Flame at the opening of the CAC Games at the National Stadium, Jamaica, in 1962

Arthur stands beside the statue,
The Athlete *at the National Stadium*

Arthur and Grace Jackson receive Order of Jamaica, 1989

Arthur aboard the M/S Starward,
participating in the Family-in-residence programme

Parson John Wint and wife Hilda, Arthur's parents. On the piano are two of Arthur's trophy cups, and the Czechoslovakian doll he won

Don Mills (right) toasts Arthur and Norma at their wedding

Norma and Arthur as they leave their wedding

Valerie, Colleen, Norma and Alison, in 1958,
a photo sent to Arthur in England

Arthur, Alison, Valerie, Spot, Norma and Colleen, summer 1962 on return to England from Independence celebrations in Jamaica

*Arthur, Colleen, grandson Lauren, Norma, granddaughter Anna
and Valerie, in Kingston, 1980*

Arthur goes down to the floor dancing "The Twist" with his grandson Lauren

Arthur stands with two Mayan young men in Antigua, Guatemala, 1968. Arthur is on the street level, the men are on the second step, and Arthur is still taller!

Arthur and Norma going to Buckingham Palace to present his diplomatic credentials

*Grandson Lauren's painting of Grandpa and himself walking in
Rock Spring, Hanover, 1977*

Valerie and Arthur at his 70th birthday party

This was also the year when the Soviets launched Sputnik, the first unmanned spacecraft. My father, uncle and I trooped outside to scan the night skies, and we were able to pick out the only light that was moving quickly – too far away to be an airplane, moving too quickly to be a star. There was a sense of excitement and wonder to be able to witness such a historical event.

In September of 1957 there was a horrendous train crash near the town of Kendal, Manchester, killing about 200 and injuring another 700. It was the worst train accident in Jamaica's history, and it shook all Jamaicans. A call went out for blood donors to help the injured, and so all the adults at Beechwood Avenue heeded the call. As a child, not quite six yet, I didn't understand how deeply affected they all were, but some sense of the horror filtered through to me, and it's one of my very clear memories.

On a more pleasant note, one of the joys of our life was to go swimming on a Sunday morning. We would sometimes go to the Rockfort Mineral Baths, with its slightly sulphuric smell and cloudy, healing water. More often we would find a spot on the beach along the open ocean side of the Palisadoes Road, the main road from Kingston to Port Royal. Nowadays I look at that stretch of coast and marvel that we swam there, as it is a very rough shoreline with dark sand and big waves. However, my father was a strong swimmer – in fact, not many people know that he had to make the choice between swimming and running. He would take me out in the waves and have me kick my legs and move my arms, pretending to swim.

Often on Sunday afternoons, after a nap and a cup of tea, we would pile into our car and drive up to Hope

Botanical Gardens near the University. My best friend Ann usually came with us. We would walk around the pond feeding the ducks, look at the orchids in the orchid house, walk on the stepping-stones through the stream, then buy ice cream and listen to the military band playing at the bandstand. Sometimes I would sit on my father's lap and 'drive' the car.

By early fall 1957 mother was again pregnant, this time with my baby sister Colleen. In early 1958 my father left Jamaica to return to England to study for his Fellowship in surgery. I clearly remember the night he left: my mother was putting me to bed and I started to cry – I would have been just six then – saying that I wanted my Daddy. My mother was also weeping and saying she wanted him too. Today she does not remember this, but it is very clear in my mind. It is one of the few times I've ever seen my rather restrained mother expressing emotion.

Colleen was born in April 1958, and it would be more than a year before we saw my father again. However, my mother kept in close touch with him through letters, sending many photographs to show Arthur his growing family. Alison, the chubby toddler, with a dimple on one cheek, and with a sly look as, dressed only in a diaper she went to the kitchen in search of the chicken leg she had been promised. Baby Colleen, who was nearly bald when she was born, and who was walking before she was nine months. I was the skinny, knobbly-kneed seven-year-old in the nurse's outfit my Daddy sent me from England for my birthday.

It made perfect sense for my mother to stay in Jamaica through her pregnancy and Colleen's first year. She was living in a family household, which gave her much-needed physical and moral support, she had a good job, and I was doing well in school. Before my father left, my mother learned how to drive, so that she would not have to depend on others while he was away. Meanwhile my father had the time to establish himself in his new hospital and find an appropriate home for his family. However, it was the first of a series of long separations that my parents endured 'for the good of the family.'

Kilrea: Life in Northern England – The Emergence of Arthur the Family Man and Surgeon

Children can be very resilient, and I don't think I was any different. Apart from crying for my Daddy on the night he left in early 1958, I don't remember missing him – my life continued more or less unchanged. My mother, on the other hand, missed him terribly, as she raised three small children on her own. She would be separated from my father for more than a year, and during that time her brothers and extended family kept much of the loneliness at bay, but there was never any question that she would join her husband in England. Our return to England signalled a period during which my father developed not only as a doctor and surgeon, but also as a family man, and my relationship with him deepened.

My father had gone to study for a Fellowship in Surgery at the University of Manchester, and was working at Altrincham General Hospital as a resident or 'Houseman' as they are known in the British system. Altrincham (pronounced *All-tring-um*) is a bedroom community an easy train ride just south of Manchester. Before we joined him, my father found a house that suited us perfectly – across the road from the hospital and the market, and close to schools, shopping and public transport. He had written to my mother in Jamaica describing this house and its amenities, as well as the fact that there were a few lovely parks nearby.

My mother packed up all three children and left the security and familiarity of the home at Beechwood Avenue in the spring of 1959. In those days, there was no direct flight from Kingston to London, so our trip took us through New York, Gander in Newfoundland, Shannon in Ireland, and finally to London. It was quite the ordeal travelling with three young children, but we arrived safely in London, where my father met us. We spent about a month in the flat at Philbeach Gardens, which my parents still owned at this stage, waiting for our new home to be ready. When my father saw us he marvelled at how Alison and I had grown, and he joked that Colleen's ears were a bit big – not what a doting mother wants to hear! She pointed out to him that she would have more balance in her face when her hair was longer. While we were in London, my father fell right into the domestic life of looking after three daughters – even to washing nappies, something I had never seen a man do before. He was clearly very happy to finally have his family back together, as we were to have him back in our lives.

We travelled by train from London up to Manchester and on to Altrincham. I remember it took three London taxis to take all of us as well as our luggage to the train station. My mother recounts that when we were ready to leave for the station, Colleen (one year old) and Alison (two years old) were nowhere to be found. A frantic search ensued, and the two toddlers were found – Alison had thoughtfully taken Colleen for a walk up the road to escape the bustle of packing.

Our new home was called 'Kilrea,' on Market Street in Altrincham, Cheshire, and we lived there from 1959–63. Altrincham is the original home of a man named 'Tring,' and the name translates as 'Tring's High Home.' 'Kilrea' is the house about which I have the most memories – I was seven years old when we moved there. Although my memories of my father during these years are sporadic, almost like snapshots, nevertheless his presence was constant, and I felt we were a 'real' family at last – mother, father and children all living in the same place. This was a sort of golden time for me.

When we arrived at our new house, Claire Schofield met us. She was a nurse from the hospital, and she and her husband Harry had become close friends of my father. She has remained a lifelong friend of my mother. Claire – or Auntie Claire, as I came to know her – had helped my father get the house ready for us, and had prepared a typical north of England 'high tea.' This was the first time I was to taste Mandarin Oranges, and to this day they remind me of Auntie Claire.

'Kilrea' was a semi-detached red-brick structure, with two living floors, a cellar, and an attic. In the other half of the house lived a young family with four young daughters. Our garden was beautiful, with a lilac tree and lots of shrubbery, daffodils and tulips in the spring, hollyhocks and peonies in summer, apples in autumn and holly berries in winter. We had two lawn areas and a long walkway, so I spent much of my spare time playing by myself out there. In the back lawn area I had my own personal garden where Daddy, son of the soil that he was, encouraged me to grow potatoes. It was here too, that we had our little roundabout that my sisters and I played on.

I have very vivid memories of that garden. I remember mowing the lawn with the push mower that made broad lines on the grass following the direction of mowing. We used to play in the shrubbery at the front, and would climb the lilac tree in the front and the apple tree in the back. I would play ball against the outhouse wall, batting the ball with my bare hand and imagining I was the greatest Wimbledon player.

Most of all I remember my scooter. My father bought it from the auction house up the road where he had bought most of our household furniture. Daddy – with my expert help – cleaned and oiled it, and we painted it bright post-box red. I spent hours on that scooter, riding up and down the walkway. I also rode it to do errands for my mother. I loved that scooter. I never got a bike, for which I wished ardently with every birthday and Christmas, but that scooter was a joy. Later, when I got my dog Spot, I would put the loop of his leash over the handlebars, and he'd go shopping too, trotting happily along beside me.

When you entered the front door of 'Kilrea,' you were in the hallway that ran past the living room and playroom to the breakfast room at the back. On the left was a coat stand (from the auction house) with a little mural of tiles along the back, telling the story of 'The House That Jack Built.' On the right was the door to the living room. It was here that our piano resided – a big, old, converted player piano on which I had my first lessons. Auntie Claire was an accomplished pianist, and she would play at birthday parties, wonderful sing-alongs led by my father with his baritone voice. A player piano is a self-playing piano, using interchangeable, 'punched-hole' paper rolls with popular songs of the times. After the 1930s, with the rise in popularity of radios and gramophones, interest in the player piano waned. Our piano had been converted from a player piano back to a 'regular' piano.

Our television was in the living room, and we watched only in the evenings. Daddy and I would always watch 'Sea Hunt' together when he was home (starring Lloyd Bridges, who solved underwater crimes), as well as 'Emergency Ward 10' and 'Doctor Kildare.' I don't recall what he thought about the medical aspect of these shows. At eight years old that didn't matter – for me it was enough that he and I watched together. I do remember the excitement in summer 1962 when my parents and I watched the first ever trans-Atlantic television broadcast via the Telstar communications satellite: President John Kennedy giving a press conference from the White House in Washington. We think nothing of such transmissions today, but 50 years ago this was a huge and important endeavour. A British pop group called the Tornadoes even made a record called *Telstar* that was on the hit parade.

These years we spent in Altrincham were in the midst of the Cold War, the state of conflict, tension, suspicion and competition between the United States of America and the former Union of Soviet Socialist Republics (USSR) from the mid-1940s to the early 1990s. The space race was part of the ongoing competition between the two superpowers, and the Sputnik satellite we had watched from our garden on Beechwood Avenue in 1957 was part of that race. In 1960, the Russians sent dogs into space, and then in 1961 the first human, Soviet cosmonaut Yuri Gagarin, orbited Earth for 108 minutes. Less than a month later, American Alan Shepard followed, and the race to put the first human on the Moon was on. This competition, this rivalry, captured the imagination of everyone, including my parents and me, as we followed the developments.

At the height of the Cold War in the early 1960s, all Britain was gripped by an unpleasant affair of illicit love and espionage involving the Secretary of State for War John Profumo, showgirl Christine Keeler, and Yevgeny 'Eugene' Ivanov, a senior naval attaché to the Soviet embassy in London, thought to be a spy. The scandal forced Profumo to resign, and the affair severely damaged the reputation of Prime Minister Harold Macmillan's government. Macmillan himself would resign a few months later owing to ill health. At about the same time, Patrice Lumumba, the first legally elected prime minister of the Republic of Congo, was imprisoned and later murdered. These political intrigues meant nothing to me at the time – I was too young to understand – but the names swirled around me as my parents and their friends discussed them, and I could not help but notice.

What I did understand was the pop culture that was growing. These were the years of the Beatles' first forays onto the pop charts, and my parents and I were ardent fans long before they reached the US, especially since they were from Liverpool, not that far from Manchester. This was also when the extremely popular and long-running – still running – TV soap opera 'Coronation Street' began, set in a fictitious area of Manchester close to our home. Shortly after it began in late 1960, I met the actresses who played battleaxe Ena Sharples (Violet Carson) and the 'tart with a heart' Elsie Tanner (Patricia Phoenix), when they made a promotional visit to my school.

Next to the living room was the formal dining room with its own exit – but we used it as our playroom. It was here that I had my dollhouse – also bought at the auction house up the street. I collected my father's old matchboxes and cigarette boxes and bits of old fabric, which I used to make furniture for the dollhouse. It was in this room, too, that the Kilrea Drama Club was born. This is a club I began when I was eight, drawing some of the neighbourhood children in to put on plays, with the proud, enthusiastic support of my father and mother. A neighbour down the street, Mrs Lord, had some experience in amateur dramatics, so she helped us find a play, rehearse it and put it on. Our first (and only) production was a play about pirates. We got all dressed up in costumes from various attics and closets, and performed our play for parents and friends who actually paid money. We were even written up in the local newspaper, the *Altrincham Guardian*. The club members took a vote and decided to donate the money we made to a nearby old folks' home, and my father helped us deliver the donation. After that production, we tried to get another one going, but unfortunately the interest had faded.

At the end of the hall was the entrance to the breakfast room. This was where we did most of our living and all of our eating, and where my father studied at night. It was a big, warm, welcoming room next to the kitchen, with an old stove that we'd had converted to a gas fireplace. Daddy's seat at the table was next to the radio and our rather exceptional toaster. The toast did not merely pop up; it popped right out, so Daddy's job was to catch the toast before it hit the floor. He developed a knack for knowing exactly when it would pop out, and his big, steady hand would always be waiting. On the wall next to the fireplace was a tall cupboard we called the larder, where we kept all the non-perishable foods and the huge bottle of ascorbic acid tablets Daddy gave us every morning to stave off winter colds. Here also was the bag of shillings for the gas metre. The gas fire, the stove and the hot water were powered by gas that came into the house via a metre. The use of the gas was paid by feeding shillings into the metre, similar to a parking metre. Off the breakfast room at the very back of the house was the kitchen. I remember it as being somewhat small, and there was a brown, circular mark on the ceiling directly above the stove, the impression of the cover of a pressure cooker that had blown off.

My strongest memory of my mother during these years is of her working in this kitchen and wearing a 'pinny,' a pinafore or apron that covered her housedress. This was quite a change from her upbringing as a middle class urban Jamaican girl, and later a career woman and householder with a staff of her own. Her job while we were in England was to look after Daddy and the children. She did all the housework in 'Kilrea,' and made all our meals. There was no concept of 'take-out' then, nor were there disposable paper diapers. Although she used rubber gloves to wash dishes and diapers, I recall her hands being so rough and chapped that sometimes they were downright raw. Daddy would bring special cream home from the hospital for her to use.

My mother loved to cook, but with all the other housework to do, she simplified this by pre-planning the week's meals. On Sundays for lunch we usually had Jamaican rice and peas and either roast chicken or roast beef with Yorkshire pudding and vegetables. Weekday meals were simple – pot roast, fish fingers. Saturdays were informal – sandwiches, perhaps, or luncheon meat. I remember luncheon meat – 'Spam' – because I would carve it into designs with my knife. Early in our years at 'Kilrea,' my mother baked a lemon meringue pie for dessert one Sunday evening. I loved it so much that every Sunday after that we had lemon meringue pie for dessert. My father's favourite meal was steak and kidney pie, but I didn't like that myself.

Although my mother was the housekeeper and cook, it was my father who taught me to cook scrambled eggs. We would go into the kitchen on a Sunday morning and whip our eggs with a little milk until they were super-frothy. We cooked them in butter in a saucepan, not a frying pan, until they were almost done, then we turned off the fire and let them finish cooking on their own. We liked them soft, with a little salt and pepper on top.

Opposite the door to the living room was the staircase to the second floor. Once, when we had only lived in the house for a short while, my baby sister Colleen fell down the stairs. Daddy happened to be standing at the bottom, and he leapt up to catch her. He saved her, but in doing so, knocked out two of the railings. They were never replaced and remained that way until we left in 1963.

Upstairs at the front of the house was my parent's room, and next to it was the room I shared with my sisters for most of the four years in England. They had a bunk bed – Alison slept on the top bunk along with her panda bear.

I had a little single bed under the window overlooking our lawn and the Conservative Lawn Bowling Club next door. I would watch the old men play there for ages. It was in this bed that I did most of my reading, for I was a true bookworm. I used my pocket money to buy myself a little flashlight, and unknown to my parents I'd like to think, I would read under the covers long after I was supposed to be asleep. Many of the books I devoured in this way were hand-me-downs from Auntie Claire's daughter, Susan, who was several years older than me.

In our bedroom was a dresser on which we would sit in the mornings as my mother combed our hair. I remember Alison in particular having a difficult time, as her hair was harder to comb. We also had a heater in the room, and my mother would hang our school clothes over it to warm them up on cold winter mornings. On Sunday nights, my father would gather all our school shoes and polish them himself, in preparation for the coming week.

At the end of the hall, directly ahead of the top of the stairs, was my father's study. He worked in here when he was studying for exams. He also slept in this room when he was 'on call' for the emergency department at Altrincham General Hospital, rather than sleeping at the hospital as the other on-call residents would have done. There was a phone in this room, and as we lived just across the road from the hospital, he could be up and out in no time. He would simply pull his trousers over his pyjamas, grab his coat and run across to the Casualty Department. We lived in an area with many factories, so there were many emergencies. My mother tells the story of one particular occasion:

> A Sister (senior nurse) told me one day how it had been when there had been a big accident. 'Casualty was all bits and pieces today, Norma. The place looked like just what you see on the telly. Arthur came in and in no time restored some sort of order. One patient didn't want to be treated by a black man, but Arthur just went ahead with his work.' Most of these tales were told to me by others, not by him. It was good to hear how he was getting on – his head full of common sense, and his size twelve shoes firmly planted on the ground.

My father found it a struggle to manage both his studies and his work at the hospital, and unfortunately failed his primary exam. This setback was understandably upsetting for him – four years of work and he hadn't qualified as a surgeon. Four years away from his beloved Jamaica and still he couldn't go home yet. He therefore took a year off to focus on his studies, and worked as an anatomy demonstrator at Manchester University. At the end of the year he returned to Altrincham General, and had benefitted greatly from the year away. He went to Dublin to re-sit his exams and this time was successful. He passed all his exams, and was now qualified as a Fellow of the Royal College of Surgeons. He could now add the designation 'FRCS' after his name, and he could return to Jamaica, head held high.

After he finished his surgical studies and qualified, he no longer needed his study. Unknown to me, my parents had redecorated and refurnished it for my eleventh birthday. When I got home from school that day, I went up to the room I had shared with my sisters, but my bed and clothes were gone. I was really scared, not being the most well-behaved daughter. Had I been so naughty that they were going to send me away? I asked Mummy what had happened, and she told me to look for my things. I found them in 'Daddy's study.' While I was at school and in the evenings after I was in bed, my father and mother had completely redecorated the room. There was new wallpaper on the walls – stripes on three walls, blue roses on the fourth – and the wood trim around the fireplace, door and window had been painted the same blue as the roses. There was a new wardrobe and chest of drawers, painted white, a little scroll-top desk, and my bed with a brand new quilt on it. I was absolutely ecstatic! My own room! It was something I had always wanted but never thought it would actually happen. Now I could escape from my pesky sisters.

Christmas at 'Kilrea' was magical. My mother would handcraft gifts for us: she once knit a whole outfit for a doll for my sister. My father seemed to have more time at Christmas, so he would often be involved in the conspiracies surrounding presents for us and helping us get presents for Mummy, and he would take us to the carolling in the children's ward of the hospital each year, but best of all were Christmas mornings.

On Christmas Eve night, Daddy would bank the coal fire in the living room by putting on lots of coals before going to bed. The fire would stay hot all night, and in the morning there would be a wonderful warmth and glowing coals waiting for us as we came in to open our presents.

That fire has become a metaphor for love with me today – a blazing fire is wonderful and exciting but dies quickly, while a fire whose coals have been banked and are hot and glowing lasts a long time.

Our Christmas tree would stand on a table in the bay window of the living room. We never received so many gifts as in the first year we were there – they completely hid the table and flowed onto the floor. Many of the gifts were chocolates or games. I once received a card game called *Lexicon*. This was a crossword game similar to *Scrabble*, and Daddy and I played endlessly together – setting me up for a lifetime love affair with words.

Another Christmas gift was a record player that could play not only 78-rpm records, but also the newer 45s and 33s. Along with the record player was a selection of 45-rpm records including Chubby Checker's 'Let's Twist Again,' Harry Belafonte's 'Mary's Boy Child,' Brenda Lee's 'Rockin' Around the Christmas Tree,' and 'Bachelor Boy' by Cliff Richard. I was really excited that year to finally have some records, as I was starting to listen to pop music on the radio. We had seen Chubby Checker on television, and so Daddy, Mummy and I taught ourselves to do the 'Twist' – Daddy and I went down so low to the floor that we weren't able to get up again, and collapsed on the floor laughing together.

The summer that I was eight, I desperately wanted to get a dog. We had searched around our area but could not find one suitable. When my Aunt Jean and Uncle Chappie came and took me with them on holiday to London, we went to the Battersea Dogs' Home, but still to no avail. I was very sad. However, Auntie Claire came to the rescue

– a friend of hers had a litter of puppies and we were able to get one. My little dog Spot was a cross between a fox terrier and an English sheepdog – small, black and white with a very curly tail. I was ecstatic, and he would be my companion for years.

For two years in a row when I was nine and ten, we rented a camper van and went to Wales on holiday during the school's Whitsun break (about seven weeks after Easter). We stayed at a B&B in Llanfairfechan in North Wales, run by – who else in Wales – a Mrs Jones. She was a little white-haired lady who couldn't have been more friendly and gracious. After all these years, both holidays have run into one in my mind.

There was great excitement over the camper van – in those days we didn't own a car, and travelled everywhere by foot, bus or train. So the van was quite a luxury. We boarded our little dog Spot in a kennel and headed out.

I don't remember asking, 'Are we there yet?' but Wales was a long drive from northern Cheshire, so I wouldn't be surprised if we weren't a bit fractious. Eventually, however, we crested a hill and came in sight of the sea. Alison, who was only four and a half that first year, piped up from the back seat with 'What's that blue thing out there?' My parents and I all laughed, having forgotten that she was only two when she left Jamaica, and so would not remember what the sea looked like.

We loved Wales. My parents would comment more than once that it reminded them of Jamaica, of Portland in particular, with the steep mountains reaching right down to the sea. We went for long walks, the most memorable being our four-mile hike up to Aber Lake. The landscape was wild and beautiful, with bare rocky crags, heather-covered slopes and bubbling streams. Daddy carried Colleen up on his high shoulders most of the way, and we were very proud of Alison, as she was able to do the entire hike on her own. At some point one year, my mother met some stinging nettles and ended up with a major skin irritation on both legs that somewhat spoiled the vacation for her.

These two vacations were among the few precious times we were all together without work or school being a factor. My memories of my father during that time are of his presence, and of his playfulness. I remember sitting in Mrs Jones's living room window, trying to draw a picture of Puffin Island just off the coast. He helped and encouraged me to keep going. I never became an artist, but he always encouraged my creative side. Several times at 'Kilrea,' we got oil-paint-by-numbers sets as gifts, and my father and I would always work at them together on the kitchen table. Of course, his paintings turned out much better than mine, which tended towards the muddy.

Back in Wales, we spent hours playing on the beach – Daddy throwing a ball, chasing us, wading in the water that was too frigid for anything more than that. The beach itself was shingle at high tide, but when the tide went out, it pulled back from its pebbly coast to reveal hundreds of yards of sand so that you could almost walk to Puffin Island. This phenomenon of the tide receding so far was a miracle to me: in Jamaica the difference between high and low tide is a matter of perhaps six feet. My father and I would wander out on the sand, and sometimes we would find little tidal pools with strange creatures stranded there.

We bought a Welsh phrase book, and my father, mother and I would try to pronounce this very difficult language, with the help of Mrs Jones. Ever since those holidays, for as long as we lived at home, my mother always told us goodnight in Welsh: 'Nos da,' she would say to my sisters, as she tucked them in at night.

When you went out through our front gate at 'Kilrea' on Market Street, you'd see Altrincham General Hospital across the road, a large, red-brick building. Next to it on your left was the Market from which the street got its name. Every Saturday, my mother would send me across with a straw basket and a shopping list. There were one or two vendors who had come to know us who served me. I would take the fruits and vegetables back home, and then head out again, this time on my red scooter and with my dog Spot, his leash over the handlebars. My mission now was to buy 'Mother's Pride' bread and other items from the grocer's around the corner.

Once my chores were done I was free. My friend Judith, who lived nearby, and her little dog Bobby, would join Spot and me for long, rambling walks in the woods and countryside around Altrincham. Springtime would inevitably find us in Bluebell Wood, and we'd come home with arms full of bluebells that died very quickly, to our chagrin.

My parents encouraged our explorations. This was in the days before cell phones or pagers, and the thought of sexual predators or muggers never crossed their minds. Or I don't think they did. Judith and I and the dogs wandered for hours. Occasionally we got lost and came home late and in trouble with our parents – but never in danger. That age of innocence has died.

In 1962, while we were still living in Altrincham, Jamaica became independent from Great Britain.

Immediately following the Independence celebrations, Kingston was host to the Central American and Caribbean Games. Both events were to take place in the brand new National Stadium. The Jamaican government invited my father and mother to attend as special guests, and they chose to take me with them. They were excited and very proud to be Jamaicans at this time. Although they were far away, Jamaica was nevertheless home, to which they would always return, and her welfare was of great importance to them.

Jamaica was only one of many countries that gained independence from their colonial 'masters' in the early 1960s: Singapore in 1959; Cyprus and several French and Belgian colonies in Africa in 1960; Uganda, Tanganyika, Western Samoa, Jamaica, Trinidad and Tobago, Algeria, Burundi in 1962; and Kenya in 1963. Most of these countries, like Jamaica, achieved independence through negotiation rather than through violent revolution. Those countries that were British colonies retained a relationship with Britain and with each other as members of the British Commonwealth.

In 1962 the short-lived West Indies Federation came to an end. Jamaica withdrew following a referendum in 1961, and Trinidad and Tobago followed suit. Without the two largest territories, the Federation could not hold, so it was disbanded. Jamaica held a General Election in May 1962, ousting Norman Manley and sending Alexander Bustamante and his Jamaica Labour Party to power: he then led the country to Independence from Britain on August 6 that year. Trinidad and Tobago also held elections, and moved on to their own Independence on August 31.

About two weeks before we were due to leave England, Alison came home from school with 12 chicken pox spots. Colleen quickly followed suit. We were worried that I would come down with it too, and not be able to go to Jamaica, but the spots held off. Alison and Colleen went to stay with Auntie Claire, we boarded Spot, and the three of us flew off to Jamaica.

We arrived at Kingston's Palisadoes Airport – as the Norman Manley International Airport was known then – and my mother's brother Chappie met us. We stayed with him and Auntie Jean. It had been three years since we had been in Jamaica, four years for Daddy. For me, this was a third of my life. Of course, I had memories of Jamaica, of friends and family, and my mother always cooked Jamaican style – rice and peas on Sunday, lots of seasoning in her meat – but the life there was unfamiliar to me. Not to mention the accent! I had become used to the Cheshire accent, and had one myself. So this was a major adventure for me.

The first night's dinner at the Marshes we were given chocho (chayote) stuffed with ground meat. I had no idea what I was eating, and thought I was expected to eat everything – after all, my mother had taught me to eat everything on my plate, but the chocho skin was tough, and I couldn't chew it. What was I to do? Then I looked around and noticed that none of the adults were eating the skin. What a relief!

The Marshes' home was party central. In those days, Jamaicans still had the habit of dropping by for drinks unannounced, usually in the evening after dinner. The arrival of my parents after such a long absence was cause for many of these impromptu get-togethers, as well as several more formal ones. My memory is of the adults talking and drinking late into the night, discussing the usual politics, with Uncle Derry probably playing his familiar role of devil's advocate.

My father had been invited to Jamaica partly to celebrate Independence, but also to be part of the official opening of the brand new National Stadium, along with Herb McKenley, Les Laing and George Rhoden – the Helsinki Quartet who had so spectacularly put Jamaica on the world athletic map in 1952. Before leaving England, my father had travelled to London a few times to pose for a major sculpture being undertaken by Jamaican artist Alvin Marriott. The work was based on an award-winning photograph of my father pushing off from the blocks, and would stand at the entrance to the National Stadium.

On Saturday, August 4, our old family friend Winnie Hewitt picked us up and we headed out for the Stadium. The traffic was bumper-to-bumper, so Winnie took a shortcut through someone's circular driveway, and as we re-entered traffic, we passed a car carrying Norman Manley. Winnie leaned out the window and greeted him as 'My Premier.' She was referring to the fact that Manley had lost out on becoming the first Prime Minister of Independent Jamaica to his rival Alexander Bustamante. I have to admit that at ten years old this meant nothing to me at the time, but I have remembered this odd greeting all these years.

We pushed our way through the heavy traffic, and when the policeman directing traffic stopped us, Winnie declared, 'I have Dr Arthur Wint here. He has to get to the Stadium to open it.' The cop immediately hopped on his motorbike, hit the siren, and escorted us through all the cars, right down to the Stadium. (Heaven knows what happened to the traffic he was supposed to be directing!) Needless to say, I was thrilled! I had no idea my father was so well known, or so important – quite an eye-opener.

When we got to the Stadium, there was a ceremony of dedication. My father and the other athletes stood underneath a statue that had been covered with a cloth. At a signal, together they cut a cord, and the cloth fell away, unveiling the magnificent statue, which was now called *The Athlete*.

This beautiful work of art has been the symbol of Jamaican athletics ever since. It stands at the front of the Stadium, with one toe pushing off the base and the body, every muscle taut, thrusting forward from that toe. It brings to mind a spring rapidly uncoiling, caught and frozen in time. The expression in the face is of intense concentration, mind and body completely in tune with each other as they focus on a common goal.

That night, Saturday, August 4, 1962 was the official Independence ceremony at the Stadium, during which the Union Jack was lowered and the new Jamaican flag raised for the first time. Princess Margaret presided over the festivities, and of course, there was much pomp and ceremony. I remember feeling proud when the new National Anthem was played, and I noted in my travel journal at the time 'we saw some children dancing Jamaican dances on the grass. It had been raining, and every step they took they splashed.' Later on, we oohed and aahed to the wonderful fireworks display.

Monday, August 6 was the actual Independence Day. There was a big float parade through downtown Kingston, and a flag-raising at St Andrew High School, where Winnie's daughter, my friend Ann, was a student. I noted in my journal:

> First the Headmistress gave a talk to the pupils about Independence, then we all got Independence cups, badges and flags. We all went out to see the flag raised. Two of the St Andrews Girl Guides pulled down the Union Jack and put up the Jamaican flag, or at least tried to, but it got stuck and they had to hold it out flat.

My parents, Winnie, Ann and I went to the Independence parade together. While we were waiting for the floats to come by, we noticed a young mother in front of us chastising her little son for fussing. My father stepped in and chastised her himself, breaking into broad Jamaican Patois saying, 'Yu nuh see seh makka jook him?' (Don't you see that a thorn has pricked him?) My father was first of all a man of the people, and this little incident was my first inkling of this side of him.

It was quite a revelation for me to see my father in his native environment, speaking his language, and being fêted by the people to whom he meant so much, and who meant so much to him. His celebrity did not change my relationship with him, but it opened my eyes to a different aspect of his life and personality.

While at the parade, I noticed a pimple on my arm that kept itching. I thought at first it was just a mosquito bite, but by the time I was home, I had developed a lot more than the 12 chicken pox spots Alison had. I was sick, and couldn't go anywhere. I was cooped up at Auntie Jean's, wiping my body with the Calomine and TCP lotions prescribed by my father – I can still smell them today. However, by the end of that week, I was no longer sick and my spots were starting to scab over, so I was allowed to go to the beach at last.

I was also well enough to go to the opening of the Ninth Central American and Caribbean Games on August 11. Three of the Helsinki Quartet – Herb McKenley, George Rhoden and Les Laing – ran one lap of the 400-metre track, and then Daddy joined them, carrying the torch. He climbed the scaffolding and lit the Games' flame. Afterwards he showed me the small burn holes in his white shorts, where the flame had sparked. I felt great pride that MY father was so important that he got to light the flame in front of the whole nation at our Independence; that he was memorialised in that lovely statue. It was probably the first time I realised he was famous.

Back in England after our trip, life picked up again. We spent one more year in Altrincham, with my father now a fully-fledged surgeon – no longer called Dr Wint in the British system, but now called Mr Wint, as surgeons are called there. This was my second year in Junior Six at school, having repeated because I was too young to move on to secondary school. This was one of the best years of my school life, and I was elected Head Girl. That year, they opened a skating rink in Altrincham, and my father took me to see my first ever ice hockey game. Later, he took me to the rink to try out skating. He, of course, had learned to skate while on his RAF training in Canada. We went slowly around the rink together several times, until finally I found the courage to skate without his help. From that time on, a group of school friends and I would go skating nearly every weekend. I still skate today, thanks to my father.

Eventually the time came for us to leave England. I simply did not want to leave: I no longer felt Jamaica was my home. I had made wonderful friends and was about to move on to the next phase in my education. I felt that my world was being torn from me. Yet there was no escaping my parents' excitement as they made the arrangements to move back home. We packed up all our things and spent our final night in England with Auntie Claire. As we left the house I felt a deep sadness, and I felt annoyed with my mother, who was worrying about whether or not she had turned off the gas stove – taking refuge in domestic trivia as she tends to do in times of stress. Auntie Claire drove us the next morning to the train that would take us to Southampton. There we boarded the *TSS Camito*, bound for Kingston via Bridgetown, Barbados and Port of Spain, Trinidad and Tobago.

As we left Southampton, we all stood on deck and said goodbye to England. The next three or so days the sea was very choppy and my mother and sisters all became seasick. My father, however, took me up on deck, into the cold, raw weather, and taught me to combat the nausea by looking out to the horizon. I felt as though I was his comrade in arms, while the rest of the family had fallen. As we sailed south, the weather cleared and the sea became very calm. I remember that as we passed near to the Azores, the sea was absolutely mirror-like, the only ripples caused by our passing.

The two weeks aboard the *Camito* were great fun. The ship was owned by Fyffes, the banana company, and would carry goods to the Islands and pick up bananas there bound for England. My little dog Spot travelled with us in a kennel on deck, and it was my job to feed him and walk him round the deck regularly. The ship carried about 100 passengers, among whom were a few children – a couple my sisters' ages, and three or four my age. We older kids spent nearly all our time together, playing quoits and shuffleboard on deck, playing endless games of *Scrabble*, watching movies, and going to a dance with our parents. It was one of the freest times I had ever experienced.

When we stopped in Bridgetown, we spent the day with a friend from my mother's time working at the University. In Port of Spain four days later, we met up with McDonald Bailey, my father's friend and rival from their days running for the Polytechnic Harriers and in the Olympics. We went to the Trinidad Hilton, and while there, according to my journal, 'we met Lady Bustamante, the Prime Minister of Jamaica's wife.'

Four days after leaving Trinidad we arrived in Kingston, met by a huge contingent of friends and family. It was early morning, and my mother describes our arrival:

> In the very early morning, on our last day aboard ship, many passengers joined us to see the ship enter Kingston Harbour. It is one of the seven best natural harbours in the world, and it was a beautiful scene at that early hour. The day was just beginning, and everywhere was still, with the sun just coming out. There were the magnificent Blue Mountains, forming a perfect background in the distance. Good to be home.

Mona Heights and Lucea

This was a very interesting time in Jamaica's political and social development. The country was only a year into its independence, with Alexander Bustamante serving as the Prime Minister. Foreign companies, which had started mining and exporting bauxite in the 1950s, were now starting to refine the ore into alumina, and Jamaica had become the biggest bauxite producer. The problems of the poor and disenfranchised were just starting to become more widely understood, and the Rastafarian movement that had started in the 1930s was becoming more prominent. It was into this dynamic time that we returned.

These years were interesting, turbulent years in Jamaica and in the wider world. In November 1963, just a few months after we arrived back in Kingston, US President John Kennedy was assassinated in Dallas, Texas. My journal entry:

> On that day, the whole world was shocked. In London, the bells of Big Ben tolled all day, a thing only done for members of the Royal Family. In Paris, French men broke down and wept in the streets. In the Vatican, Pope Paul prayed and Italy's president wept.

In June 1965, Dr Martin Luther King visited Jamaica and was given the Keys to the City of Kingston. I was so impressed with him that I copied into my journal the entire text of his acceptance speech. However, one part struck me most and has stayed with me all these years, I think now because subconsciously I realised that it echoed my father's attitude to life:

> If it falls to our luck to be street-sweepers, sweep the streets like Raphael painted pictures; sweep the streets like Michelangelo carved marble; like Shakespeare wrote poetry, and like Beethoven composed music. Sweep the streets so well that all the hosts of heaven and earth would have to pause and say, 'Here lived a great street-sweeper, he swept his job well.'

A year later, Emperor Haile Selassie of Ethiopia visited Kingston. Originally known as Ras Tafari, His Majesty is considered the reincarnation of God, or Jah, by Rastafarians and this visit was a high point in their faith. Many thousands waited at the airport, smoking ganja (marijuana, a sacrament for Rastafarians), drumming and chanting. The visit had great significance in the development of the Rastafari movement: having been outcasts in society, they now gained some respectability for the first time. Bob Marley and other artistes of various kinds were beneficiaries of this growing respectability.

When we arrived in Kingston, we headed to our new home in Mona Heights, a Government house in which we would live for two years. This is the same housing development where my uncles Chappie and Derry lived with their families. My father took up a post as surgeon at Kingston Public Hospital; I started at St Andrew High School for Girls (my mother's alma mater); Alison started at St Andrew Preparatory School; and my mother stayed home and home-schooled five-year-old Colleen, who was not able to be enrolled in St Andrew Prep at that time.

Very early in our new life we experienced what was, for me, a novelty experience: a hurricane. In early October 1963, Hurricane Flora hit southwest Haiti, then headed west to Cuba. For three days this deadly, 140mph hurricane stalled over Cuba, its path tracing a loop and causing catastrophic flooding, thousands of deaths and devastating the crops. The intense driving rains of Flora's slow movement extended to Jamaica. The island wasn't hit directly, but the eastern end was severely affected. In Kingston, we were only a month into the school term, but we had several days off due to the storm. I remember the hurricane-tracking map that was published in the *Daily Gleaner* newspaper, on which we followed Flora's progress. It amazed me when I saw the looping path over Cuba, and when I heard about the loss of life and the loss of the entire sugar crop I felt sad.

In our house on Lily Way in Mona Heights, I had my own bedroom, while my sisters continued to share. Interestingly, my room had been painted a strange orange colour, but it was mine and I loved it. I was beginning to settle into school and to make new friends, and my father continued to be a major part of my life.

One of the most vibrant memories of my father and me together, is of playing tennis at the Bustamante Children's Hospital. I had never played before, but we had avidly followed Wimbledon together while we lived in England.

I also used to hit a ball against a wall with my bare hand, pretending to be a top Wimbledon player, so tennis was a sport that definitely interested me. I never knew my father could play, but now that I've learned from talking with my Uncle Lloyd that my father was good at every sport he tried, this is not so surprising. We would go to the courts at the hospital on Saturday mornings and play a few rounds together, and I felt special to have this time with him.

A month after my twelfth birthday, I had my first ever menstrual period. When my father came home from work, my mother told him what had happened, and he came to me in my bedroom where I was doing my homework. He gave me a big hug, and said, 'Congratulations. You're a woman now.'

That Christmas Eve, as I lay in bed with my stocking hung at the end of my bed, I was just drifting off to sleep when I heard the sound of a penny whistle playing 'It Came upon a Midnight Clear.' I got up to look for the source of the music, and glimpsed my father lying on the bed with a black and gold flute in his hands. I went back to bed. When I woke up early on Christmas morning and opened my stocking, I found the usual stocking-stuffers – little toys, an apple – and a black and gold penny whistle. When I asked my father about his having played it the night before, he said I must have been dreaming, because Santa Claus had brought the flute. To this day I remember the flute's wistful sound, and whenever I hear that Christmas Carol it brings memories of my father.

Life was not all rosy in the Wint household, however. Brewing on the horizon was another separation from my father, one that would forever change our family and would colour my own personal relationships with not only my father, but with all men. It's at about this time that I read *The Diary of Anne Frank*, and started regularly writing a diary of my own (I had sporadically kept a journal before this). One entry from June of 1964 – I was 12 then – illustrates the fear and foreboding I had about my family:

> My home life is so awful. Mummy and Daddy are always rowing and now Mummy tells me that she is fed up with Daddy. She says that he just goes ahead with everything (money-wise) and then when everything is bought and paid for, he tells her that he is £40 overdrawn from the bank. She says that whenever she tries to talk to him about it, he gets into a temper and there is a big quarrel.

> I'm just positive that this family will soon break up – either by separation or by divorce. And either way, the children are never taken away from the mother, which is what I will hate. I can't live with only Mummy. I can't live with only Daddy – I have to have both, and so do Alison and Colleen.

> I have almost everything I could want, except for a secure family. I wish to goodness that ours was a better one. I can't even think about what my friends would say if they ever separated, because I'm always raving about how wonderful my Mummy and Daddy are.

When I was about 13 or 14, I believed my parents would actually divorce. One night I overheard my mother talking to him on the phone. She was asking, 'Are we staying together for the children's sake?' – words that sounded as though she was at her wits' end and that perhaps they should divorce. I knew that upheaval was in the air and I was terrified, but it never happened. In reality, they were separated to all intents and purposes – he lived in Lucea, Hanover, in the far west end of the Island, while we lived in Kingston. We had a life completely separate from his, as his was from ours, but we were still a family. I left home at 17, and never lived with my family again.

Years later as an older teenager I asked my father about these quarrels. He told me that they were actually quite healthy and were a way of periodically releasing steam: if they didn't do this, the frustrations would build up and somebody would simply explode. He tried to reassure me that quarrelling did not necessarily mean the family was breaking up. I never got used to them, and to this day I fear these kinds of blow-ups. They always made me fear my parents would break up and this led to a lifelong tendency in me to freeze in the face of conflict. Things that happen in your youth can truly affect your entire life and worldview.

After two years living on Lily Way, my parents bought a house on Geranium Path, also in Mona Heights. We were thrilled to be able to own our home, and I was particularly thrilled with my new bedroom – it was a beautiful shade of pale blue, very calming and serene, a good antidote to my volatile temperament and my old orange bedroom. Our house had a large, gracious verandah with a yellow awning keeping it shady and cool, and the garden was lovely. When we pulled the awning up, we had a breathtaking view of Jack's Hill, and behind it the glorious Blue Mountains.

For me, the golden time of my life that had started in England was about to come to an end – my father moved away for his job. The fears I had written about at 12 were being fulfilled. I was 13 years old, and this was the last time I lived with my father. He took on a 'locum' – substituting for another doctor – in the town of Falmouth on the north coast of Jamaica. This is the town his mother was from, so he had a few friends and relatives there. He lived in a historic Georgian house where we visited him from time to time.

I never questioned my father's move to Falmouth. I believed – hoped – it would be temporary, but this was not to be, as he was subsequently offered the post of Medical Officer in Lucea, Hanover, in the west end of the island. There were great discussions between my parents as to whether the whole family should move to Lucea or stay in Kingston. The ultimate decision was that my mother would stay in Kingston with the children so we could go to the 'better' schools there. This was not a decision made lightly, and in retrospect I don't believe it was the best. I believe it irreparably damaged the relationship between my parents, and put a stress on my mother that she was not entirely equipped to deal with – three daughters to raise essentially on her own, one of them just entering the rebellious teens. For our education I believe it was definitely the right decision, but I believe their marriage suffered, and never truly recovered.

So Daddy moved to Lucea. He was the surgeon at the general hospital in Lucea, and on specific days he had clinics in nearby Green Island and other towns. He rented a big old two-storey house, with space on the ground floor for a small private practice, and a verandah around two sides of the upper storey. On the other side of the street was the Presbyterian manse, at the top of a grassy hill sloping down to a level. We would sometimes roll down that hill, and sometimes we'd watch the older boys playing cricket on the level section at the bottom. Next door to Daddy's house were the Clackens, relatives of Miss Clacken who had taught my sisters and me, and who would later teach my own children at St Andrew Prep School. The Clackens had two sons, the elder Dwight and Harry, who was about my age. They were of a Christian sect that were considered to be very extreme, and weren't allowed to spend time with us – we could only talk over the fence.

Daddy's housekeeper in Lucea was Judith Dixon. At the time I knew Miss Judith she was quite old. In fact, she had looked after Daddy as a young boy in his parents' house. She was quite a character, and loved Daddy dearly. I remember her delicious coconut pies and her thick grey hair.

We fell into a routine of making the five-hour drive down to Lucea on holidays, while my father would come into Kingston for a couple of weekends each month. On occasion he would surprise us by just showing up in time for dinner, spending the night and then driving back then next day. He missed his family. We missed him.

Sometimes our holidays and long weekends were just our immediate family, but often we would take friends and relatives along with us.

We would usually go to three different beaches on those weekends. There was the small, almost private beach four miles out of Lucea called Bull Bay. You had to park on the road and climb down a rocky path to the sandy cove.

Doctor's Cave in Montego Bay was another spot we'd visit. This is a tourist beach very close to the hotels, always crowded. We would drive the 25 miles into Montego Bay soon after breakfast, and spend the whole day there, returning in time for dinner. I would invariably get sunburnt at Doctor's Cave Beach. My memories are vague ones fuelled by a photograph of my two younger cousins, Richard and Warwick, at about ages five and three, standing on the beach in their water wings.

Negril is the beach that holds for me the most poignant memories – seven miles of exquisite white sand and turquoise waters sheltered by on offshore reef at the extreme western end of the island. We would go to Negril Sands Beach Club, which was owned and operated by Hans and Elinor Gubler, dear friends of my father. Elinor came from a local family that owned a sugar estate, and the Swiss-born Hans had been an engineer on her father's estate. He had learned English at high school in Switzerland, but had become fluent after migrating to Jamaica – he spoke a very picturesque Jamaican English and Patois with a strong Swiss accent.

We would spend entire days at Negril Sands, taking a picnic lunch with us. Often it was just Mummy and us kids, as Daddy still had his various clinics around the parish of Hanover. Sometimes, though, he'd manage to get away early and would join us.

Negril Sands had a main bar area which was a big round structure with a thatched roof, the bar at one side and tables in the centre. On the beach were several thatched huts with hammocks. We would arrive early enough to snag a hut for ourselves. On one occasion, we had spent the entire day at the beach and had driven all the way back to Lucea. We were unpacking the car when someone said, 'Where's

Spot?' He always travelled with us from Kingston, sitting up on the ledge behind the back seat. We realised we had left him at Negril, so we all climbed into Daddy's car and drove back to the beach, worried about our little dog. However, when we got there, Spot was sitting under the thatched hut where we had spent the day, just waiting for us.

On another occasion, when my friends my friends Gail and Ann were there, we were on Negril Beach at dusk and noticed tiny shellfish coming in on the waves and burying themselves in the sand at the water's edge. Gail, who had lived in St Lucia, said the St Lucians called these 'Ahi' and they were good to eat. So we got some containers, filled them with seawater, and started collecting ahi. We had to keep them alive until they were cooked. We took them home, boiled them until their shells opened, and then we painstakingly picked the tiny bits of flesh from each shell. All in all, we got enough ahi (plus lots of fine sand) to spread on one piece of toast each – not much, but they were quite tasty. We would eat our gourmet treats while playing a very cut-throat version of Rummy with Daddy at the kitchen table.

When Alison's friend Robin and our cousin Tracy were with us, the four girls put on a play one night for our entertainment. It had to do with a queen in her palace, with Robin as the queen and Alison as a servant. At one point, Alison had us in stitches, when she came out dusting the palace walls with the toilet brush, saying 'It's so hot in the palace today.' We all applauded the young actresses, but I later realised there was an interesting comment on race in Jamaica here: Robin, the queen, was very light-skinned, pass-for-white, while Alison, the servant, was probably the darkest-skinned of the foursome.

Daddy had a private practice on the ground floor of the Lucea house, so at certain times on certain days patients would come to see him. He was very strict about his office hours. He would get quite angry if someone came after hours, unless it was an emergency. More than once, I witnessed his anger at the person who arrived at three in the morning, who had already been sick for two days and who was only now coming to the doctor. I've actually seen him throw a shoe out the window at someone: he was very impatient with anyone who did not respect his clinic hours. He would send these people to the hospital. Yet I've also heard him tell of the baby he delivered – or 'caught' – in that surgery: the mother was barely able to make it from the waiting room into the clinic before the baby started to come, and he basically had to stoop down to catch it before it hit the floor. I also remember his ethical dilemma, one that I'm sure many doctors face, of having to work to save the life of a prisoner who had been sentenced to death.

He was the only doctor for miles around, so at some point most people came to him. It's happened to me more than once that as an adult living in Canada I've met former patients of his. 'He saved my life,' one might say, or 'He looked after my old mother in her final days.'

One of the highlights of our trips to Lucea would be our annual day trip to Black River in St Elizabeth, for the St Elizabeth Horticultural Show that was usually held close to Easter. Both my parents loved flowers, and they grew beautiful plants in their gardens as well as in pots. So we would head out for the day to look at all the fascinating plants at this show. There was one occasion when they held a dog show as well, and at the last minute we decided to enter Spot in the 'Mixed Breed' section. He had never been in a show before, but a very poised Alison led him around the ring, and to our surprise he won!

My father lived in the old place for several years, and then in the early 1970s he acquired a parcel of land at the top of the road on which the old house stood, and built a home for himself – later his father would join him there. He had the house designed to separate his surgery from his living space. It was on a sloping corner lot, so the surgery had its entrance from one street, while the residence was entered from the adjacent street. The surgery was situated on the lower level of the structure, with its own exterior door, but my father could enter it from within the house. By the time it was built, I was living in Canada so I never had a strong tie to the place. Eventually, my father bought another property in Portland, in the northwestern end of the island, with the plan that each of his daughters would inherit one of the three properties he now owned. This plan never did come to fruition, however, as he ended up selling both the Portland property and the house in Lucea.

My father made a tangible impact on Lucea during the years that he lived there – from 1965 to 1974. When he first moved to this rural town, some of his new neighbours were concerned that such a famous man would be snobbish, but they quickly discovered how down-to-earth and practical he really was. They found that he was able to communicate with anyone he encountered, having an ability to move from speaking standard English to Jamaican patois with ease. They also found that he did not take himself too seriously, and could be quite playful. He soon became an integral part of the Hanover community.

He was selected as chairman of the board of governors of the Green Island Secondary School, and along with then principal Simon Clarke, became curious as to why several of the students were not achieving academically and were always tired. Initially they thought that these children were eating too many carbohydrates – yams, sweet potatoes, rice – and not getting sufficient protein. My father surveyed the children and to his astonishment discovered that they were all the children of fishermen, and were actually eating a lot of protein. They were, paradoxically, not eating enough carbohydrates. As a result of this study, a breakfast programme was instituted at Green Island Secondary, high in both proteins and carbohydrates, and the problem of tired students seemed to have been solved. In later years, when I was a teacher at Green Island Secondary, the breakfast programme was still going strong – and I can personally state that it was very delicious too!

My father was instrumental in starting the Hanover Parish Choir, in which he sang baritone. His good friend Ruby, who was also in the choir, recalls:

> The choir was a brainchild of Dr Wint's and a lot of fun. The members consisted of people from the community in Lucea and some of the teachers at Green Island. As a matter of fact, the choir director was the music teacher at Green Island. In the initial stages a lot of us could not drive and we did not have cars. Dr Wint would drive around and pick up people and take us to choir practice. When he couldn't make it he would arrange a carpool. Eventually as more people joined the choir we were

able to arrange our own transportation. We would
meet every week and sing our hearts out. We even
performed in public a couple of times. Today I can't
listen to 'Ave Verum' without a feeling of nostalgia.

His impact extended beyond the choir to other aspects
of life in the local community. Ruby describes his reaction
when a group of young people complained about how
boring it was in Lucea:

'Dr Wint, this place is so boring,' we would whine.
'Can't you do something?'

Then he would look at us and impatiently
say, 'Missis, I am one tired donkey, I can't do
everything.' After that we would laughingly refer
to him as the tired donkey. Anyway, no matter how
tired he was he always tried to make things better
in Lucea. Apart from the Hanover Parish Choir, he
was actively involved in the Lucea Flower Show.
He loved flowers and plants and he and others
would work diligently to make sure the annual
shows were a success.

Arthur also tried to keep the Lucea Country Club
alive. He and others would plan dinners and dances.
He also served on the board of the Hanover Parish
Library. No matter what he did he made sure
young and old alike were included.

I was not directly privy to these aspects of my father's
life. I must have been aware somewhat of his non-medical
community activities, but my life was in Kingston – I had
no real connection to Lucea except to visit my father. I
not only had school to contend with, but also the angst,
the rebellion, and the very active social life of an urban

teenager. I nevertheless savoured the times I had with my father, either alone with him or as part of the family.

There weren't many times that my father and I spent extended time alone together. There were a few isolated instances as a child, when we played together, or when he took me somewhere. Yet for the most part, I shared my father with his work, with the rest of the immediate family, and with other people. However, for one whole week of my life I got to have him completely to myself.

When I was 16, the Mona Heights Citizens' Association held a big, fundraising bingo in the Mona Heights Community Centre. It was one of those rare occasions when my father was in Kingston, so the whole family went, but to be honest, I wasn't particularly interested in playing – certainly not for the little piddly prizes they were offering. I was way too cool for that. So I decided to go across the road to the home of a friend, and hung out at his place for a while with a few other friends. We could hear the goings-on clearly from his house, so at a certain point we realised that the grand prize for the bingo was a trip for a week to Guatemala City. My friend and I decided to return to play for that prize.

Daddy bought us each two cards, and we began. The game was going along nicely, until it came down to three final numbers. My friend and I had one of those numbers in common, and that was called first. The tension was palpable. Now it was down to the wire between him and me. One of us was going to win the jackpot. They called my number! I screamed. I yelled. I jumped up and down. I had never won anything before! I was going to Guatemala!

Of course, at 16, there was no way I would be allowed to go alone, and the prize was a trip for one. So it was, that in the first week of August 1968, Daddy and I went to Guatemala together for a week. It was probably the only time that he and I had ever been entirely alone together for more than a few hours.

We flew on a small airline that for a short while plied between Kingston and Guatemala City. We were never really sure why they started that route at all – there's not much traffic between Jamaica and Guatemala, but we headed off, quite excited. I had been taking Spanish for a year, so I took along my dictionary. One memory of the flight is that Daddy taught me to play poker – we played matches for most of the way to Guatemala City.

We had looked up Guatemala in the encyclopaedia and learned a little about the place. When we arrived, however, I think several things struck us immediately: how short the people were, the military on foot patrol through the city with their machine guns and *bandoleros* over their shoulders, and the many people selling lottery tickets by the side of the road. We were impressed with the city, its grid layout – *calles* in one direction, *avenidas* in the other – and its Spanish colonial architecture. The hotel we stayed in was top notch.

I didn't know it at the time, but Guatemala was in the midst of an extremely turbulent period in its history, one that has never really had much let-up. The period between 1960 and 1996 saw armed insurrection in response to the autocratic rulers. In 1966, the army began a counter insurgency campaign against the guerrillas, who then concentrated their attacks on Guatemala City, and, it is said, assassinated the US Ambassador in 1968.

Did my father have any inkling that we were heading into such potentially dangerous territory? If he did, it certainly didn't percolate through to me as any sort of fear. The sight of armed military seemed somehow romantic to me, not something to be feared. I thought I was very sophisticated, but, truth be told, I was actually very naïve. Perhaps we both were.

So, oblivious to any external threats, we decided the best way to see the country was to be true tourists. We signed up for two tours that would take us into the interior and to the Pacific coast, with various stops along the way. Ours was a small group in a minivan: our driver, two young German women, an American man, and the two of us.

Driving through the Guatemalan countryside showed us many similarities with Jamaica, as well as many differences.

Like Jamaica, poverty was rampant, but it was curious for us to see poor people who were not black, and while we were accustomed to seeing the wealthy as white, in Jamaica in the 1960s there was also a sizeable black and brown middle and upper class. We did not see this in Guatemala – we saw poor Mayans and wealthy whites. Yet everything was so novel to me, that there was no sense of outrage at the inequality. My sense of outrage came during the months following this trip as I grew more aware of the inequities in Jamaican society and became passionate about wanting to change the situation.

One big difference we noticed in Guatemala was the way in which the country people carried heavy loads.

Like Jamaicans, they used their head to carry, but whereas Jamaicans carry the load right on top of their head, the Mayans used a band across their foreheads supporting the load that rested on their back. At times we saw them bent almost double under the weight. I shudder to think what this did to their spines! At least Jamaicans have to stand quite erect when carrying a load on their head, no matter the weight of the load.

My father was very impressed by the communal washing area we saw in one rural village. There were washtubs laid out in a circle underneath a simple roof with open sides. The women were then able to come and do their laundry with clean running water, in a communal setting where they could chat with each other. He thought that this layout would be perfect for rural Jamaica, especially in areas where the women still went to the river to wash. It allowed for the socialising that goes with river laundry, but that is lost when running water comes into the house.

Among the various places we visited, was the incredibly beautiful Lake Atitlán in the Guatemalan Highlands. The lake was formed following a giant eruption and is surrounded by three dormant volcanoes. The German girls, Daddy and I decided to have a swim in the lake. This meant diving off a dock and swimming to a raft. The Germans went in first, and then I dived and hit water so cold it took my breath away – at an altitude of more than 5,100 feet and with the lake about 1,100 feet deep, how could I have ever have thought it could be warm enough for me? As soon as I surfaced, I turned to tell my father not to come in, but he was already mid-air! We swam to the raft, but of course, we then had to return, in that freezing cold water – one of the hardest things I had ever done. I must say, the Germans did not seem to mind the temperature at all!

We went to the Pacific Coast and that was more like what we were used to in Jamaica. It was hot and sunny, and the ocean was warm. In Jamaica, the beaches near Kingston are of black sand, as was this one. However, this was black volcanic sand that glistened in the sun. The beach was fairly steep so that there were sizeable waves. Daddy, the German women and I played in those waves, bodysurfing onto the beach, laughing as the waves tumbled us about. At one point, a wave caught me just the wrong way, turned me over, and I slid onto the beach on my hip, earning a beautiful, very painful long scrape from the deceptively sharp volcanic sand that looked so soft and smooth.

One of the towns in which we stopped was Antigua, which had a church at either end of a huge, crowded square, with a market in it. We wandered in the market and in the churches, and at some point we acquired two young Mayan boys of about 16 or 17, who had decided to be our guides. You have to picture how striking we must have looked to them, two tall, black people. In a photo, we see one of the boys standing on the second step of one of the churches, while my father is on the street level and he is still a head taller than the young man! We must have appeared like giants to them, and they had likely never seen black people before.

An image I will never forget was on our way back to the city from the Pacific Coast, as we were driving along a ridge, with the mountain falling away on both sides of the road. It was dusk, and we were travelling due north, and to our left was the setting sun – one of those breathtaking sunsets with brilliant golds and reds and yellows. To the east, on our right, the full moon was just rising. Sun and moon were precisely opposite to each other, so the moon itself was resplendent, reflecting the incredible sunset. It is a view that has haunted me ever since. I am particularly grateful that I had the chance to share this unique experience with my father.

A couple of days after we arrived in Guatemala City, a group of French-speaking Africans arrived. Naturally, as fellow black people and residents of the hotel, we struck up an acquaintance with them, me speaking in my best high-school French. They were Les Ballets Africains from Guinée, on tour in Central America and the Caribbean. It tickled me at the time, but they thought my father and I were husband and wife! Did they think I looked so mature? I have never really given it much thought over the years, but looking back now I realise that many African men marry women much younger than them. My father was also quite young looking at 48. We shared several meals with them, and of course we went to their performance. As luck would have it, they were scheduled to visit Jamaica in a few weeks, so we made a point of visiting with them at that time, and of going to see their performance at Carib Theatre in Kingston. It was my first experience of Africans, and I was gratified to learn that my French was reasonably acceptable.

One day we had been out walking in Guatemala City, and passed a cinema that was screening *To Sir With Love* with Sidney Poitier. I had already seen the film and loved it, but my father hadn't. So two Jamaicans went to see this very British film, subtitled in Spanish, in Guatemala City. My father really enjoyed it. It no doubt evoked memories of living in London, and some of the problems he encountered there – in particular the racism that manifested itself whenever he looked for lodging, or with some of his athletics teammates.

This trip was to a place so unusual for us – we were used to England, the US, and Europe – that we bought some unique mementos. For myself, I got a *huipil*, the Guatemalan version of a poncho, hand-woven in bright, almost psychedelic colours, and which I wore at my first wedding. I proudly bargained, in Spanish, with one of the waitresses in the hotel restaurant, for a beautiful traditional embroidered blouse such as the one she wore. We also bought a tablecloth and napkins, and a couple of tray cloths that my mother still uses, and a set of carved wooden plates that today, more than 30 years later, are still in daily use.

Thinking back on the week in Guatemala, I realise that it was not only a lovely trip, but also a time in which my father and I developed a friendship that went beyond the father-daughter relationship. He had always been distant in one way or another – geographically distant most of the time, actually. He had been around when I was a child, but because of his studies and the weird hours of his work, his presence was more general than specific in my life. Also because he did not live with us during my teen years, I did not really get to know him as I was maturing. My mother was the constant presence. She was the one who involved herself in our schools, who drove us around, who dealt with discipline, and with whom I had a most difficult relationship. My father became the romantic 'other.' This trip allowed me to shed the rose-coloured glasses, to see and accept him more as a real person, warts and all, and to absorb from him many positive traits that have stayed with me.

For two or three summers when I was in my teens, we went on holiday for a week up in the Blue Mountains above Kingston. We would stay in a Ministry of Agriculture house in Newcastle usually, and the last time we stayed in a house at Hardwar Gap, outside Newcastle.

I loved these holidays. It was one of the few times the whole family was together. Newcastle, at 3,000+ feet above sea-level, was originally a British Army garrison – no doubt selected because it has a wonderful strategic view of Kingston and its harbour, but more so because the air is more salubrious and cool than on the St Andrew plains. Today it is a Jamaica Defence Force training base. Surrounding it are houses that were originally officers' homes. In the late 1960s when we went there, the Ministry of Agriculture owned them, and one could rent them. We would go for long hikes on the trails marked on the maps that hung in the Newcastle cottages. Our hikes would take us higher up the mountain in various directions. While on our various hikes, as we slogged slowly up the steep paths, we would often be overtaken by soldiers running up, then down the mountain with packs on their backs. We were in awe of their strength and stamina.

One particular walk took us to Clifton Mount, an old Great House from the heyday of the famous Blue Mountain coffee. The entrance to the property was a beautiful rose garden that fascinated both my parents, great gardeners as they were, and featured a sundial in the middle. The house contained many beautiful Jamaican antiques, of which the most memorable was the bathtub. This was carved from a single cottonwood tree, in the same way that the old-time fishermen used to carve out their canoes. It had a drain-hole but no taps – the servants would have filled it with buckets of water.

We loved the change in climate that the mountains offered us. As you drive up towards Newcastle from Papine, there is a point where the atmosphere changes. It's quite tangible, this change, and there is an aroma, the scent of some plant or tree growing at that altitude – perhaps eucalyptus or pine – that will eternally evoke our times in the Blue Mountains. Also, at that elevation, one finds the solitaire, a bird seldom seen, but whose cry is poignant and heartbreaking.

While we didn't spend a lot of time in the mountains, we all loved it and cherished this special time together. I don't recall any strife at those times – no quarrels between my parents, none between me and my mother – the memory is of fun and harmony.

The last time we went together to the mountains, was to Hardwar Gap, about four miles outside of Newcastle. It's spelled Hardwar but pronounced Hardware – named I believe for the town in Uttar Pradesh, Northern India. This was 1969, the last summer I lived in Jamaica with my parents, immediately after the end of high school. I was 17, had just completed the dreaded 'A' Level exams, and had my driver's license. At that time I was starting to spread my wings and become a bit more independent. In a few weeks I would be heading off on my first solo adventure, as an exchange student to Iceland.

Music evokes those days, along with the driving and the surreptitious cigarettes. The music from *Hair* was in the air, specifically 'Let the Sun Shine In/Aquarius' and 'Good Morning Starshine.' I recall 'Starshine' playing one morning as I sat alone at dawn in that exquisite mountain garden.

During these times, my father treated me more as a grown-up than my mother did. This is not surprising, as he had not had to deal on a daily basis with the difficult and rebellious teenager I had been.

At Hardwar Gap we would go on long, rambling walks, as we had at Newcastle. Here, however, our walks took us downhill rather than up – forgetting that we would have to climb back up at the end of our adventure. We would follow the various trails that inevitably led to one stream or another. My sisters, my father and I set about building dams across these streams, or exploring upstream. We would clamber over the rocks, slipping into the water. These areas are generally dark and moist, with ferns growing on the banks, and of course, the invisible solitaire somewhere nearby.

A month after this last holiday in the mountains, I left for my year in Iceland. When I returned the following summer, I was only home for a month before leaving again for university in Toronto, Canada. The first few months in Toronto were extremely difficult for me, and all I wanted was to come home to Jamaica. This was not an option, so I dealt with my unhappiness by having a relationship with one of my fellow students and becoming pregnant. My mother was devastated, and rather than deal with this on the phone, she came to Canada to discuss with me the ramifications of having a baby. I was adamant that I was not giving up this baby, and so my boyfriend Tony and I got married that May.

My father came to our very Bohemian wedding, as did Tony's father and my Aunts Monica and Jean and Uncle Derry. My mother did not come, but she made our cake and sent Anthuriums for me to carry. The ceremony was held outdoors in a field by a stream with a few of our good friends, and was great fun. Both our fathers loved to sing, and Tony's father also played the guitar, so we had a little singsong out there in the field. I was thrilled that Daddy was there, but saddened that my mother was not. I felt judged by her absence.

Our beautiful daughter Anna was born that summer of 1971, and that Christmas and the next we took her to Jamaica. Her Grandpa fell in love with her, as did the rest of the family. Our son Lauren was born in late spring of 1974, and he too became very close to his Grandpa.

My leaving high school meant the divergence of my story from my father's. He continued to live and contribute to life in Lucea; my mother and sisters continued to spend time with him there; and he continued to visit them in Kingston. However, another change was on the horizon, another turn that would take my parents back to England and into an entirely new life. This change was precipitated by the election in 1972 of Michael Manley as Prime Minister of Jamaica.

The Diplomat

In the mid-1960s following Jamaica's Independence, up to the early 1970s, there was an increasingly wide gap within Jamaican society between the 'haves' and the 'have-nots.' Illiteracy was rampant; unemployment was endemic; 'rude boys' were governing in the ghetto areas of Kingston; 'sufferers' were voicing their disaffection with the status quo. The right-wing Jamaica Labour Party had been in power since Independence 1962, initially under Sir Alexander Bustamante, and succeeded by Sir Donald Sangster and Hugh Shearer.

These were also years of change and turmoil around the world. In the US, the Kennedy brothers, John and Robert, had been assassinated, as were Civil Rights leader Martin Luther King and Black Power activist Malcolm X. The country was at war in Vietnam, a war that was extremely unpopular at home, with anti-war demonstrations a regular occurrence. In Eastern Europe, the former USSR invaded the country formerly known as Czechoslovakia. The Cold War raged between the Communist Eastern Bloc and China, and the US and its allies. South Africa was under the apartheid thumb and the anti-apartheid leader, Nelson Mandela, was in jail.

In the US, the Hippie culture had arisen, espousing peace and love, and decrying the war. At the same time, the Rastafarian religion was coming to the fore in Jamaica, also espousing peace and love. Yet good, upstanding, middle class Jamaicans were very wary of this group of mainly working class, bearded people, who worshipped Emperor Haile Selassie of Ethiopia, and who smoked ganja (marijuana) as a sacrament. Not until Bob Marley swept onto the international music scene in the mid-1970s with his activist lyrics, was Rastafari more widely accepted.

In Jamaica, American Black Power was influencing the students at the University of the West Indies (UWI), in the high schools, and in the wider population. The people were tired of being dominated by an elite that was controlled by the former British colonialists and increasingly by the new colonialists, the Americans. Symbols of Black Power could be seen in the Afro hairdos, Dashiki shirts, and in music such as 'Say It Loud! I'm Black and I'm Proud,' and 'Young, Gifted and Black.' White and light-skinned Jamaicans started feeling less sure of themselves as this movement gained momentum.

Racial and class tensions simmered, kept just barely under the surface. In October 1968, these tensions bubbled over into a demonstration that became a riot in Kingston. Walter Rodney, a Guyanese lecturer at the University, was denied re-entry to Jamaica and declared *persona non grata*. His travels to the USSR and Cuba, and his study of Rastafarianism and Marxism, had unnerved the Jamaican Government, which was very anxious not to upset their US puppetmasters. On this occasion, Rodney was returning to Kingston from a Black Writers' conference in Montreal, Canada. When he was denied re-entry in to the island, University students led a demonstration, closing down the Mona campus of UWI. Students and sympathisers – me among them – marched to the Prime Minister's residence and then to the parliament building, gathering demonstrators along the way. Luckily I had a very strict mother who insisted that I be home at a certain time, because eventually, as these things happen, the event got out of hand, and a series of increasingly violent riots ensued, involving tear gas and looting. 'The seeming hopelessness of the period was captured in the Ethiopians' chart buster of the day, "Everything Crash,"' commented Arnold Bertram in the *Sunday Gleaner*, April 9, 2006.

> *Ev'ryting crash, ev'ryting crash*
> *Firemen strike*
> *Watermen strike*
> *Telephone Company too*
> *Down to the policemen too.*
>
> *Every day carry bucket to the well,*
> *One day the bucket-bottom mus' drop out*
> *Every day carry bucket to the well,*
> *One day the bucket-bottom mus' drop out*
> *Ev'ryting crash.*

It is against this backdrop that the intelligent, eloquent, and charismatic Michael Manley and the People's National Party (PNP) campaigned to a landslide victory in the 1972 general election. Manley was a proponent of Democratic Socialism, with a shift to the left, calling on the people's social consciousness, proposing social justice and trying to bring together people of all races, classes and cultures. He courted relationships with Cuba, various African nations, and the USSR. He denounced US imperialism, and this scared many middle class Jamaicans into migrating to North America as they felt that Manley would take their property away. He also inspired the more nationalistic – myself included – to return home from our studies abroad and to participate in this gigantic socio-political project. I was married and studying in Toronto at the time, and on the night of the election, my husband, a Jamaican friend and I were following the results on the radio. When it became clear that Manley and the PNP had won, we were euphoric. That's when we decided to return to Jamaica when our studies were over, and so in 1975 my husband and I came to be teachers at Green Island Secondary School, where my father had been Chairman of the Board, and lived in Lucea where he had once also lived.

Shortly after coming to power, Michael Manley approached my father and asked him to consider leaving medicine for a while to act as Jamaica's High Commissioner to the UK. Now Arthur Wint was probably one of most unlikely people to be considered for a diplomatic post. He had no experience in that field – he cared little for the trappings of power, and had absolutely no interest in the social aspects of such a job. Yet he cared passionately about his Jamaican people, whether they happened to be in Jamaica or not.

There was much soul-searching following Manley's overture. The family came together for tea at our home in Mona Heights – my two sisters, my mother's two brothers and their wives and children – to discuss the prospect. After deep debate my father accepted Manley's proposal.

Not everyone was convinced that he was the right person for the job. Some people thought it was a good idea to send him, others said they should have sent someone who was a career diplomat. 'But the main criticism,' says my mother, 'was that doctors could not be spared at this time. When is a time when doctors can be spared anyhow? We are always short of doctors.'

So it was that in 1974, my father embarked for England once again – not this time as a fighter pilot, nor as a doctor, but in his third career as a diplomat. He was taking over the portfolio from Sir Lawrence Lindo, a light-skinned, upper class Jamaican. Lindo was an 'old-school' style diplomat – in fact, he had been head of the Diplomatic Corps – who was about to retire. It was believed that Lindo, although he meant well, was no longer the right kind of person for the job and it was time for a change. The average Jamaican living in the UK felt that the High Commission was not serving their needs, and Manley felt there needed to be someone in place who could bridge gaps within the community. He approached my father deliberately, knowing that he would be respected not only by the Jamaicans in Britain, but also by the other diplomats and by the English in general: he was known in all these circles. As my mother put it later:

> There was a kind of rift – there were over 300,000 Jamaicans in England, and there was a kind of rift between the High Commission and the ordinary Jamaican people in England. They felt that they weren't getting enough attention. And Michael felt that someone like Arthur, whose name was well known in England already, and popular with all different classes of people, and Jamaicans as well, he would be able to mend the rift, which he did. He did a lot of community work in England, not just the social side of being a High Commissioner

and attending a lot of dinners and cocktail parties and so on, but he went to all the different parts of the country and met with the community people, Jamaican community people, who were striving to make a life for themselves, which is what Michael wanted, and which he did, with great success, so that when he left, people had no end of farewell parties because they were so happy with him.

Arthur had an advantage in dealing with Jamaicans in Britain, in that he was very much a man of the people. He was black, as were most of the constituents he dealt with. He was the son of a rural minister, and so he grew up going to country schools and running around the countryside – literally running. He then became a rural doctor, and so he had a lot of contact with the very people whose relatives had emigrated from Jamaica to England.

He also found that some of what he did as a doctor was useful as a High Commissioner. A doctor has to be a good listener, because patients came to him supposedly for something else, but they really wanted to say what was in their heart. So in the diplomatic service, by being a good listener he was able to solve many of the problems that people brought to him.

One area of British life that particularly irked my father was the education system and the way in which Jamaican students were treated as second class citizens. He fought hard to try to reverse this. These were the years following massive migration of black West Indians to Britain seeking work in the 1950s, the Notting Hill riots in the summer 1958, of Black Power in the 1960s, and consequent to all of this, racial fear and suspicion between white English people, and black immigrants and their British-born children. The teachers and principals were finding many of the Jamaican students very hard to handle, and as a result a good number of teachers were not giving their students the appropriate opportunities or tools to move ahead and excel academically. Their premise was that the students were substandard, but rather than work with them to bring them up to standard, they would just push them off and send them to the trade schools, saying 'You will be good working with your hands.' Of course not all teachers were like this, but as my mother says, 'It was very much like *To Sir with Love*.' My father was very disillusioned with this aspect of British life and did what he could to change things by bringing the inequalities to the attention of the school authorities and the media. The women of the Jamaican diplomatic community also helped by donating textbooks to schools where there were many Jamaican students.

A great deal of his time in Britain was taken up with helping Jamaican community groups all over the country in one way or another – attending fundraisers, helping with the school situation, generally looking after his fellow Jamaicans. Another part of his life was as the Jamaican Government's representative to the UK, Sweden and Denmark. He had to look after Jamaica's trade deals with these countries, a job for which he admitted he was by no means qualified, but he had people around him who were qualified, and who were able to advise him.

The one aspect of the job that he detested was the social side – tea with the Queen and having to dress up in what he called his 'monkey suit' with top hat, for example. Can you imagine Daddy, six-foot-six tall wearing a top hat! Some things he simply refused to do: he went once to the Derby, that prestigious horse race, but never went again. Similarly, he refused to attend the ultra-chic Ascot races. According to my mother, he said, 'If I go up to the Derby, I'd rather go out on the grounds where the gypsies and the ordinary people are. That would be my speed, and watch the races there.' As High Commissioner, however, he would have to dress up in his 'monkey suit' and sit up in the stand. So he went just the once. My mother, on the other hand, loved the social life. She liked to attend these functions, and loved to entertain in her own home. My father went along with the agenda, but left to his own devices, he would have hopped on a plane bound for Jamaica and never left again.

Another aspect of the job that he did not like was being an agent for the Government and not being able to make decisions without consultation. He had been a doctor and surgeon for many years, working mainly on his own and making his own decisions. In addition, he was not much of a political animal, but in this position he had to defer to his political bosses and he found this irksome. So when his four years were up, he let it be known that he would not be continuing. He wanted to return home, to return to his people and his medical practice.

My sisters were in their teen years when my father was posted to Britain. They both finished high school there, with Alison going on to study medicine at the same college where our father had studied and where I was born, St Bartholomew's Hospital. Colleen returned to Jamaica not long after leaving high school, joining my husband Tony and me in teaching at Green Island Secondary before going to UWI. During the years when my family was in Britain,

I was studying in Toronto, and then in 1975 moved back to Jamaica with my young family, lured by Manley's vision of a better Jamaica. I never visited England and was not witness to my father's day to day life as a diplomat. However, I saw him on his downtime, when he escaped from this artificial life and returned to rural Jamaica to stay with us. At these times he would go to visit his good friends Elinor and Hans at their beach club in Negril, and let all the stress of the job dissipate over some good Jamaican rum and a few raucous rounds of dominoes.

On one particular visit, Elinor had a brunch for some friends. She introduced us to a lovely drinking game. Each person pours a glass of rosé wine. They turn to the person next to them, link arms, and look into each other's eyes, making the following interchange:

> First person says, 'I looks towards you.'
> The other replies, 'I catches your eye.'
> First person says, 'I nods my head.'
> The other replies, 'I likewise bow.'

With arms linked, they drink their wine and so it goes around the circle.

My father and I took part in this silly, special ritual, and in a very tangible way it made us closer. I recall us walking on the beach and talking about some of the things in our hearts at the time – his frustrations with life in England, my frustrations with my own life as my marriage to Tony had started to unravel. We were able to talk in ways that we never had before, more as friends than as father and daughter.

We had not lived together since I was 13, and I had not been able to visit while they were in London, so catching up with him on these visits to Jamaica became very important to me. He found the diplomatic life stressful, making this downtime in rural Jamaica vital to his well-being – like getting a hit from a drug that would sustain him until the next visit. He would stay with us in our house in Rock Spring, Hanover, sleeping on the extra-long bed we had acquired somewhere along the way. It was during these hiatuses that he grew close to my children, the first of his grandchildren. There is a very touching photograph that we cherish in our family, of my immensely tall father walking down one track of the gravel driveway with my tiny son – he was about two years old – following behind him. The two are walking away from the camera, in perfect step with each other. As an art student later in life, my son – now also immensely tall – did an acrylic painting of that photograph, which hangs in pride of place in his grandmother's living room. At his wedding, I brought tears to his eyes – and those of many others – as I told the gathering about this image and the special love between grandfather and grandson.

The four years of my father's tour of duty in the UK saw my parents and sisters together once more, after the years apart while he worked in Lucea. My mother and both sisters relished this time: my mother later commented that 'there has to be a lot of love in a marriage for it to survive all these separations and we were happy to be together again.'

The Last Return Home

After my father's four-year tour of duty as High Commissioner to the UK, my parents returned to Jamaica in 1978. He had given the diplomatic world a good shot, but it was not his passion, nor did it really play to his strengths. His first love was the practice of medicine among his beloved rural Jamaicans, so he requested a rural post when he returned to the island.

The global political and social climates, during which my father had served in the UK, were fraught with violence and unrest. The late 1970s and early 1980s were very tumultuous years in the world at large, in the Caribbean, and in Jamaica. Internationally, these years were marked by the Soviet invasion of Afghanistan, the Iran-Iraq war, the hostage crisis at the US embassy in Tehran, the mass suicides of Jim Jones and his followers in Guyana, and the deepening debt crisis in developing countries leading to severe financial restrictions and hardships. In 1980 Zimbabwe became independent in what was seen as a triumph of negotiation over armed revolution, while there were military coups in Nigeria and major violence in Lebanon, as well as war between Great Britain and Argentina over the Falkland Islands. There were several assassinations and attempted assassinations: former Beatle John Lennon, Egyptian leader Anwar Sadat, Indian Prime

Minister Indira Gandhi and Swedish Prime Minister Olaf Palme were all killed.

Closer to home, major events were taking place on the tiny island of Grenada. Maurice Bishop and his socialist New Jewel Movement, aligned with Cuba and other Communist countries, made the US very nervous. Under Bishop, the fortunes of the Grenadian people had begun to improve – health care, education, and employment – but the hardline Marxists, led by former Deputy Prime Minister Bernard Coard, felt that Bishop was too moderate. So, on October 13, 1983, the Grenadian Army, controlled by Coard, seized power in a bloody coup. He deposed Bishop, who was eventually executed along with two of his cabinet and dozens of protesters. The severity of the violence, coupled with Coard's hardline Marxism, caused deep concern among neighbouring Caribbean nations, as well as in Washington, DC and so the Organisation of Eastern Caribbean States asked the US, Jamaica and Barbados to help. As a result, in the early morning of October 25, 1983, the United States invaded the island of Grenada – population 100,000. The initial invasion force met stiff resistance, but the island quickly fell under American control. Under American occupation, life for Grenadians deteriorated rapidly, as the US tightened its grip on their daily lives, and all the Cuban advisors and workers were expelled.

Meanwhile, in Jamaica, Prime Minister Manley's Democratic Socialist experiment had failed. Elections were announced for October 30, 1980, and in the months leading up to those elections, there was tremendous 'tribal warfare' between factions of the incumbent left-leaning

People's National Party (PNP) and the opposition Jamaica Labour Party (JLP) led by pro-capitalist, pro-US Edward Seaga.

This culture of violence around political parties and elections was not new to Jamaica: it had begun when the two-party system started in the 1940s, and had become stronger in the lead-up to the 1976 elections, which saw Manley and the PNP return to power. The violence that preceded the 1980 elections was unparalleled, however. Gangs allegedly armed by both parties fought for control of urban constituencies, resulting in more than 800 Jamaicans killed. While the murder rate in Jamaica has long been high, Jamaicans were particularly shocked by the violence at that time, and many sought to leave. Canadian friends of mine urged me to leave Jamaica at the time, but I had no intention of doing so.

As a result of this violence and believing that his government would be overthrown by destabilisation – thought by many to have been promoted by the US – Manley declared a State of Emergency that lasted from June 1976, until 1977. In 1978, Bob Marley held the One Love Peace Concert at the National Stadium in Kingston in an effort to bring the opposing factions of the PNP and JLP together peacefully. The concert peaked during the performance of 'Jammin,' when Marley joined the hands of political rivals Michael Manley and Edward Seaga and called for unity. Unfortunately, the concert did little to reduce the violence, and it would not be until Marley's funeral three years later that Manley and Seaga would be seen amicably together in public.

After winning the election in 1980, Seaga quickly expelled the Cuban ambassador, and other Cubans working on the island – workers who had built a number of schools and colleges, and doctors who supported the healthcare system. Following the invasion of Grenada in 1983, Seaga called a snap election that was boycotted by the PNP, so that the JLP now held all 60 seats in Parliament.

It was into this unsettled climate that my parents returned. On their arrival home, they went to live in an apartment at Olympia Hotel near Papine, Kingston. The idea was for my father to get re-acclimated to Jamaican life, and specifically to the practice of medicine. He went to work at Kingston Public Hospital and at Bustamante Hospital for Children to hone his skills before being assigned to his new posting. He wanted a rural hospital, but my mother was adamant that they be close to Kingston. She wasn't going to be left alone again, especially now that all her daughters were out of high school and on their respective ways in life, and she wanted to be close to her extended family and the conveniences of the city. Consequently, my father accepted a post at Linstead Hospital, about an hour's drive out of the city. Initially he commuted from Kingston, until they found suitable housing in Linstead.

During the time my parents were living at Olympia, my sister Colleen was in residence at the nearby University of the West Indies. Recently separated from my first husband, I was living with my children in a flat in Mona Heights, a mere ten-minute walk away from Olympia. Most Sundays found us at Olympia for lunch, and once again my children had the opportunity to get close to their grandparents.

When the time came to move, they rented a house in Linstead belonging to a family who had emigrated during Michael Manley's government. It was situated on a hill that fell away on both sides of the house, with lovely gardens, many fruit trees, and four dogs: two Corgis and two German Shepherds. The house was long and narrow with two wings – bedrooms on one end and kitchen, dining room and living room on the other end, linked by a partially covered verandah. Most of our living was on this verandah. On weekends, my sister Colleen, my children and I would drive down to Linstead – we had great times there. My father settled back into life as a country doctor, and as the surgeon at the Linstead Hospital, while my mother went to work as the Company Secretary at a large local citrus estate.

The house was perfect for entertaining, and my mother was in her element, cooking and entertaining guests – visitors from overseas, colleagues of my father's, close friends and family. After all the guests had left on one such occasion, we sat on the step of the verandah looking out over the hill, and sang every Beatles song we could think of. Then we got our old St Andrew High School hymn book and sang every hymn we knew. Both my parents had beautiful voices that Colleen inherited, while I could hold a tune fairly respectably. My father with his rich baritone and Colleen with her alto voice provided the harmony.

My parents lived in this house for about two years, until shortly after the JLP won the 1980 elections and the owners decided very quickly to move back to Jamaica. My parents had to find new housing immediately. They found another home, also rented, but much simpler and more down to earth than the first house, and they were able to put down some roots here, making it a real home. My mother continued to entertain: she loved to have people around to cook for, to try out new recipes.

My father had returned to the soil. This house had a beautiful garden in the front, while at the back my father and Noel, the gardener and houseman, grew vegetables. They experimented with winter melon, and when our good friend Easton Lee heard about the soon-to-be-ready melon, he said that he and his wife Jean would come to the house and cook traditional Chinese Winter Melon Soup for us. They came early in the morning and started the melon on a slow fire, filling the interior with meat, spices and the scooped-out melon. That meal was truly memorable, with Pepper Steak – cooked by my father – and various other Chinese dishes to accompany the soup, as well as good friends to help enjoy it.

After one of these parties, again all the guests had left, and it was just the immediate family cleaning up. At a certain point someone turned on some rock 'n' roll music, and my father and I started to dance the 'Twist' – memories of Altrincham. I have a photograph of my father down in a squat doing the 'Twist' in the living room.

In addition to the vegetable garden and the fruit trees on the property, there was a large concrete tub near the back fence – we were never quite sure of its original purpose. Nevertheless, my father had the notion to raise fish in this tub. He equipped and stocked it according to specifications, but for some reason the fish never thrived, and unfortunately that experiment failed.

My sister, my children and I would often drive down to Linstead for the day, or would stop by on our way to or from the North Coast. For some reason I've never fathomed, my very skinny son would eat like a trooper when he was at Grandma and Grandpa's house, so I almost felt it a duty to make sure he went there at least once a month. It was during these visits, apart from the parties, that my children really grew close to their grandfather. They would walk out in the garden looking at the various plants and just chatting with Grandpa – nothing deep, merely connecting.

It was at this house in Linstead that my baby sister Colleen got married. My children and I flew down from Toronto – we had moved back there in 1985. My daughter Anna was to be bridesmaid. Our sister Alison also came from Britain with her two toddlers. Before the big day, there were of course many little niggling details to take care of, but on the day itself everything flowed beautifully. Colleen got dressed at a nearby friend's home, with my help, then Daddy came for her and they drove down together. He escorted her to the 'altar' that had been set up in the carport with flowers beautifully arranged by Easton Lee, and stood aside as her husband stepped in. The ceremony went smoothly, with most eyes on Colleen, looking so assured and beautiful. However, my eyes went to my father, who was weeping silently as his last daughter got married. His heart and mine met in those moments.

My parents did not own the house in Linstead: however they still owned the house in Mona Heights, where I had lived with my children, and where Colleen and her family subsequently also lived; there was also the house in Lucea that my father had built. Reluctantly, they sold that house, as it was not useful to them any longer. There was a small, new subdivision called Brook Green in Ocho Rios on the North Coast, where both my mother's brothers had bought houses. My parents also bought one of these, and for years this was their refuge. They would head out on a Friday and return on Sunday evening, after a lovely weekend of relaxing and taking in the beach. On long holiday weekends, all three families would congregate in Brook Green, sharing meals and good times, often with friends dropping by and discussing the affairs of the day – very reminiscent of the Beechwood Avenue days.

During the first several years that he was in Linstead, my father was the resident surgeon at the Linstead Hospital. Due to the many accidents and incidents of violence, he worked long, hard hours, and might be called out at any time of day or night. He also maintained a private practice as well, and after he retired from government service and no longer worked at the hospital, he continued this private practice. True to form, he accepted whatever payment his patients could afford – cash, produce, chickens. For a while when he first moved to Linstead, there was a Cuban doctor working with him at the hospital to lighten the load somewhat – until the Cubans were sent home. Later, an Indian doctor came on staff, Dr Khotiah, whose young family became frequent guests at our gatherings, and whose young wife taught my mother some tricks of Indian cooking.

From time to time my father had to come into the city for one reason or another, and he would invariably stop by the Mona Heights house for a quick visit. He never tarried, he couldn't wait to get back to Linstead, because 'Your city too hot for me, massa!' He was a true son of the soil.

He would head back to his cool home in the country, strip off his work clothes and put on his home 'uniform' – shorts, tee shirt and running shoes. The shorts were white, navy, or light blue, but the shirts, as I recall, were always white. Thus attired, Daddy would sit out on the verandah with his beer – cold Red Stripe in a glass that lived in the freezer – and his cigarette with the long ash falling off, and ponder life. Sometimes he would look through that day's *Gleaner* or *Star* newspaper, but usually he simply sat and looked out. My mother could never fathom this sitting for hours 'doing nothing,' and she would become quite annoyed with him. He would argue that he wasn't 'doing nothing,' but that he was, perhaps, going over a surgical procedure in his head, or a sticky case he might be dealing with – visualising as he had done years before as a world-class athlete.

Mummy would despair of him, that he didn't have a hobby. Daddy was not like Uncle Chappie, my mother's brother, who after work would read voraciously – that is, when he wasn't puttering around fixing something or making some new piece of furniture.

One of the 'sticky cases' he often had to deal with in his practice was children with dysentery, which dehydrated them severely. In North America, such children would be given a special rehydration liquid with the right amount of electrolytes. In Jamaica, however, with poverty a key factor, the rural folk simply cannot afford to buy these special fluids. There is, however, a natural product ready at hand: coconut water. It is sterile and has all the nutrients and electrolytes the small children needed, and it grows on trees all over the Island. Coconut water was the best thing, my father maintained, for babies with this ailment, and he helped many a small child recover by this simple means.

In 1988 Hurricane Gilbert struck Jamaica, but the house in Linstead stood up well. However, my parents had to do without water, electricity or telephone for several days – in fact, electricity did not come back for some weeks, and my mother had to bring home ice from her workplace, which had a generator. As a result of the hurricane, my father was not able to watch the Seoul Olympics on television, but his friend and former teammate Herb McKenley made him a videotape of the events, so he appreciated that. He was very proud of the 100-metre win by Jamaican-Canadian Ben Johnson – we talked about it on the phone – but then was completely devastated when it was learned that Johnson had tested positive for performance-enhancing drugs. I could hear it in his voice.

It was during the years in Linstead that my father, along with Professor John Golding, Leila Robinson and others, founded the Sports Medicine Association of Jamaica. They offered their services at track meets such as the very prestigious Boys' and Girls' Championships, and helped to educate coaches and athletes alike. One of the issues they could help with immediately, they discovered, was that of young athletes who were being asked to compete in the midday heat following a strenuous journey from the rural areas to Kingston, without adequate nutrition or hydration. Simple, nourishing foods and drinks could be given these athletes, and all would be well. The Sports Medicine Association is still going strong today.

A few years after moving to Linstead my father received an honorary Doctor of Letters from Loughborough

University in Britain, so he and my mother travelled to England for the ceremony, which my mother describes as 'a very fine function,' and now he could add 'D. Litt. (Hon)' after his name. Some time later, my father would be further honoured, along with several other sports greats as the first inductees in the Jamaican Sports Hall of Fame. The other honourees included Herb McKenley and the other Helsinki relay athletes, as well as the cricketers George Headley the batsman, and Alfred Valentine the spin bowler. My father spoke on behalf of all the inductees, and my mother relates that he was 'quite overcome, but managed to get through his speech.' My father would also be part of a feature article in *Sports Illustrated* magazine that looked at the phenomenon of the Jamaican sprinter and middle-distance runner. This was years before Usain Bolt and other Jamaican stars burst onto the scene in the 2008 Olympics, piquing the interest of the world media who could not fathom why Jamaicans did so well at those distances. My father and others had already blazed that trail by excelling on the world's tracks, but the media had forgotten their exploits. *Sports Illustrated* was ahead of the curve by examining the sources of this phenomenon.

My mother always made birthday cakes for the various members of the family, and would take the time to decorate them beautifully. An example of this was on my father's seventieth birthday in 1990, when she made a copy in icing of the iconic photograph that was used in creating the statue at the National Stadium – which touched my father greatly. We had a big get-together with family and close friends. At that birthday my father told me privately, 'Well, I've completed my three-score and ten. Anything after this is brawta.' 'Brawta' in Jamaican patois means 'extra.' I objected, telling him he was much too young to be thinking that way, little knowing he was right.

Not long after this celebration, my father began to ail. His prostate was being troublesome, and being the typical doctor he did not seek help. His health deteriorated until he finally had surgery to – as he put it succinctly – 'ream it out' and clear the blockage. Unfortunately, some journalist heard about the surgery and broadcast that my father had prostate cancer, which was not true. Later, the radio station had to recant, but the damage had been done, and it was a difficult time for both my parents.

Nevertheless, this illness was perhaps just the beginning of the end. He deteriorated not only physically but emotionally as well. Whenever I visited Linstead, I would sit out with him on the verandah, sometimes in companionable silence, sometimes discussing our thoughts about issues of the day. In the latter years it was at these times that he confided in me his despair about the direction that Jamaica was heading. He felt strongly that Jamaicans had lost the sense of self and self-respect they once had, and no longer had respect for others. He talked about the climate of aggression that always bubbled near the surface, erupting into violence under the slightest provocation. He spoke bitterly of young men who had no drive or focus, but who proved their manhood by fathering children they could not support financially or emotionally. He lamented the decline of amateurism in the Olympic Games, where athletes competed for financial gain and not for the joy of the sport, and that the Olympics were no longer the games of gentlemen who respected each other – the Ben Johnson doping incident only reinforced that feeling. He told me more than once that he saw no reason to keep going. To this day I feel guilt that I was not able to help him through this despair and regain his vitality.

My father had a Transient Ischemic Attack (TIA) or 'mini-stroke' while at work on Monday, October 12, 1992. Somehow, he managed to drive himself home and go to bed. He didn't say anything to anyone. When my mother came home she found him in bed, a most unusual occurrence, as he was not one to take naps. She called Dr Khotiah, the Indian doctor who worked at the Linstead Hospital, who had been Daddy's friend. They bundled him into Dr K's car and drove him to Kingston, to Medical Associates Hospital.

Colleen called me in Toronto and told me what had happened. When I asked if I should come to Jamaica, she said, 'no, let's watch and see what happens.' So each day I would get a bulletin on his condition and his treatment.

On Thursday that week, I drove with my second husband Jim up to North Bay, several hours' drive north of Toronto, for a video shoot. Jim was shooting a concert during which Canadian singer Catherine McKinnon sang a deeply moving rendition of 'Amazing Grace' that brought me to tears. It was my father's favourite hymn. Was this an omen? I left the auditorium, found a phone, and called Colleen. She said I'd better come, as things didn't look too good. I immediately started calling around looking for flights, and was able to get a booking for Sunday the October 18.

In Kingston, Colleen picked me up at the airport, and we headed straight for the hospital. When I arrived,

Daddy was very glad to see me and was mentally alert. In fact, he was too busy to talk to me right away, as he was listening to the Canada-Jamaica soccer game on the radio, and Jamaica was not doing so well. We listened along with him. He seemed in good spirits, and was able to sit in a chair for short periods of time.

After the game – which Jamaica lost – we chatted. He had a lot of phlegm on his chest, so the nurse would come in from time to time, prop him up and let him spit. Elizabeth Robinson, a physiotherapist friend of his and fellow member of the Sports Medicine Association, would also come in to tap his back to loosen the phlegm. We talked about the church service that had been held in his honour earlier that day, which Colleen and Mummy had attended. My father was also slated to receive a special award later that week. He realised he would not be able to go, so he asked Colleen to go in his stead.

The next morning, my mother and I arrived at the hospital at about 9:30 am. He was lying in the hospital bed, having difficulty breathing. The nurse sat him up so he could clear his lungs and spit. Finally he told her not to bother.

'Isn't it more comfortable for you to sit up?' I asked.

He replied, 'You makes your choices.' These were his last words to us.

The doctor came in and said that overall he was pleased with Daddy's progress. 'If he continues to get better, he should be discharged by Wednesday. However, he'll need home nursing, so go and discuss this with the hospital Matron,' he said. My mother and I went down to Matron's office and started setting things up for his discharge and subsequent home care. In hindsight I wonder if sending us away was a ruse so we would not see how bad things were.

We were gone for about half an hour. As we came up the stairs, I could see much coming and going in and out of his room, so I sat Mummy on a bench with her back to it all, but I could still see. At one point I asked what was going on, and I got some sort of evasive answer. I tried to prepare Mummy for the possibility that this was the end. I called my sister and aunt.

Finally we are allowed into his room. He has had a pulmonary embolism, and is unconscious. It is just a matter of time now. The nurse keeps him going by pumping air into him with a kind of bellows in his mouth. She keeps him going until Colleen, Jean and Chappie arrive.

Colleen kneels beside him, holds his hand and sings the John Denver song she used to sing to her children when they were babies:

> *Sunshine on my shoulder makes me happy,*
> *Sunshine on my shoulder makes me cry.*
> *Sunshine on my shoulder looks so lovely,*
> *Sunshine somehow always makes me high.*

She and I tell our father how much he is loved. We remind him of the wonderful grandchildren he is leaving behind, of how beautifully they are growing. My mother says he can't hear us. Colleen and I say of course he can. We tell him it's OK to let go now. We'll be fine. We cry as he leaves us. The nurse stops pumping. As the monitor flat lines, she turns it off. He is gone.

Last Days

I'm convinced my father decided to die. He made the choice. He was seriously ill for a week, and had been in less-than-perfect shape for more than two years. He would have absolutely hated to be bedridden and a burden in any way. In fact, I believe he probably thought he was dying when he drove home and went to bed, probably thought he would simply die alone in his own bed, with no fuss, no fanfare. His own father went the same way – collapsed in church, which had been his life – and died a week later. Similarly Daddy had a mini-stroke in his medical office, which had been his life, and died a week later. As they say in the obituaries, he died peacefully with his family at his side. Unfortunately, my sister Alison was not able to get home to Jamaica in time before he went, coming as she was from England, and was saddened that she could not see him to say goodbye.

The days following Daddy's death flew by, and I had no time to really feel anything. The government offered to give him an official funeral, which we accepted. There were therefore issues of protocol we had to follow, but still we wanted to incorporate certain elements into the service specifically for Daddy and for ourselves. My aunt Jean Marsh, my younger sister Colleen and I, and Alison when she arrived, were the ones who went into organisation mode, dealing with arranging the church, liaising with the Ministry of Foreign Affairs and others, trying to make this send off the best possible. The RAF Association desperately wanted to bugle him into and out of the church, but on this we were adamant – no bugling – our natural simplicity as a family hated the bugling idea. They were quite upset with us. We were horrified at how public it all became, and said more than once 'Daddy would have hated all this fuss.' Yet the usual response was: 'He would have hated it, but if anyone understood why it was necessary, it would have been him.'

My mother was out of it. She was in shock, quite unable at that point to deal with any of the decisions, as she was on tranquilisers most of that week.

Ann, my friend from childhood, was magnificent, in that she undertook to get the approvals necessary for cremation, and to deal with the funeral home. When they were ready for someone to make decisions, she took me there. Daddy's body was lying in state, and several people were sitting praying nearby. I never knew who these people were, but I suspect they were 'professional' mourners. Mrs Clarke, the owner of the funeral home, was quite droll about the casket: because Daddy was so tall, she had to have one specially made for him. Since he was being cremated, the casket would be re-used. 'I just hope I get another long one soon,' she quipped.

Naturally most of the talk over these few days was centred on Daddy – what he was like, anecdotes from his life. Amidst the sadness that he was gone, there was much humour and laughter. My daughter Anna in particular had a hard time with this. She couldn't understand how one could laugh when a loved one had died, but laugh we did.

Finally the day of the funeral came around, and much of it went by in a blur. I remember helping Mummy decide what to wear, and the to and fro as we tried to find the right clothes for her. Before we left for the church, I made sure my son-in-law Craig and my son Lauren, who are both rock musicians, tied their long, unruly hair into reasonably conservative ponytails.

There was much discussion – argument even – about whether Alison and Colleen's children should come to the service. They were very young at the time, ranging in age from three to six. Both mothers insisted that it was important for the children to have closure, and to witness this rite of passage. They believed that death was not something to hide from children. Some of the older relatives did not agree. Of course, the mothers prevailed, and the children attended.

We met at the Marshes' home on Aralia Drive in Mona Heights, where we were picked up by limo and driven to the beautiful Chapel at the University of the West Indies. Daddy was lying in state at the entrance to the chapel, and people were filing by, paying their last respects. I will never forget the look of total despair and sadness on my son Lauren's face as he said goodbye to Grandpa.

The funeral was beautiful, a truly fitting farewell for a truly great man. The Chapel was filled to capacity, but a TV monitor had been set up outside so the overflow crowd could see the proceedings. Among those attending were Prime Minister P.J. Patterson and Leader of the Opposition Edward Seaga, as well as other government leaders and top officials. My father's old friend and former athletic rival McDonald Bailey came from Trinidad, blind now but wanting to be part of this farewell, as did his former teammate Herb McKenley. What would have touched my father's heart more, however, were the busloads of well-wishers who had come from Lucea and from Linstead – nurses, doctors, former patients, old friends. My father had this ability to connect with people from all walks of life and those people all wanted to give him a good send-off.

One of the speakers was Mike Fennell, head of the Jamaican Olympic Association, who surprised and delighted everyone present by playing an audio recording of my father's 400-metre gold medal race at the London Olympics before he gave his eulogy.

My old friend Cecil Cooper sang one of my father's favourite songs 'The Impossible Dream,' and when the University Chapel Choir sang Handel's 'Hallelujah Chorus,' I turned to Colleen and said, 'Daddy's loving this.' However, it was the whole congregation singing 'Amazing Grace' that moved me the most. Jamaicans have a great love of music and of singing, and they will find the harmonies and counterpoints that fill out the music, and so they did with 'Amazing Grace' and the other hymns that day. The ancient limestone walls of the Chapel resonated with their harmonised voices.

The casket was carried out of the Chapel to the haunting theme from 'Chariots of Fire,' the film about track athletes whom my father knew well. The family followed behind, and when we emerged from the soft light of the Chapel into the harsh mid-afternoon sunshine, I was overwhelmed to see so many people outside, crowding the driveway and flowing up onto the surrounding lawn. Parked in the driveway was a green hearse into which they loaded the casket, and as it drove away I said quietly, 'Bye Daddy.' He was finally gone.

Now I could mourn. After the get-together at my uncle's home following the service, my husband, children and I went to my parents' cottage in Ocho Rios. This is where I finally let go and simply wailed in anguish for my father. I was angry that he left us so young, only 72 years old. His own father had lived to 96, why could Daddy not have stayed a while longer? I was sad that I would never see him again. I would never again hear his voice answer the phone when I called from Toronto, saying 'Hello darling,' angry that he wouldn't see any great grandchildren. I felt as though I was the only person in the history of the world who had lost a beloved parent, and even today, so many years on I still feel that loss.

Here was a man who had lived a fuller life than most. He had made one very questionable choice in his early years, for which he spent his entire life atoning. He excelled as a pilot in the RAF so that he was promoted to Flight Lieutenant. He excelled as a track athlete so that he won the first-ever Olympic gold medal for Jamaica. He excelled as a doctor and surgeon, caring for his patients with compassion – though not always patient himself and not suffering fools quietly. He excelled as a son of Jamaica, so that no matter how far he travelled, no matter how long he stayed away, he always returned to his country, his people, his soul's home, and to us, his three daughters, he was always, simply, Daddy.

Postscript

My father loomed large in my life. He was a tall man, a head or more above the crowd, and this holds true metaphorically also. His lifetime achievements read as if he were three or four men, not one, and the discipline he brought to these achievements was great. He was a man of the soil, the Jamaican soil, passionate about his people and his country, always returning. Yet when that country and those people seemed to him to have lost their way, he felt betrayed, and he withdrew from them. It seems that he left us before his time – still, given how many lifetimes he packed into his 72 years, perhaps it was his time. As a daughter who misses her father, however, I will never accept that. I will accept, however, the gifts he left me: the discipline (though I don't always exercise it); the sense of duty; the ability to talk and connect with anyone, regardless of their station in life; and now in my middle years, the ability to run and to help heal.

Thank you Daddy.

Arthur Wint's Statistics

Date	Location	Race	Place	Time
1938	Pan Am Games, Panama	800 metres	First – Gold	1:56.3 (Central American Record)
1943	District Services Championship, (for RAF) Brandon, Manitoba	440 yards	First – Gold	48:4.5
1946	AAA	440 yds	First – Gold	48.4
	AAA	880 yds	First – Gold	1:54.8
	Central American & Caribbean Games, Baranquilla, Colombia	880 yds	First – Gold	1:54.8
	Central American & Caribbean Games, Baranquilla, Colombia	400 metres	First – Gold	48.0
	Central American & Caribbean Games, Baranquilla, Colombia	4x400 metre relay	First – Gold	3:18.0
1948	Olympic Games, London	400 metres	First – Gold	46.2
	Olympic Games, London	800 metres	Second – Silver	1:49.5
1950	AAA	880 yds	First – Gold	1:51.6
1951	AAA	880 yds	First – Gold	1:49.6
1952	AAA	440 yds	First – Gold	48.1
	Olympic Games, Helsinki	400 metres	Fifth	
	Olympic Games, Helsinki	800 metres	Second – Silver	1:49.63
	Olympic Games, Helsinki	4x400 metre relay	First – Gold	3:03.9 WR??
1953	International Track meet, Sabina Park, Kingston